INTRODUCTION TO FIRST NATIONS MINISTRY

CENTRE FOR PENTECOSTAL THEOLOGY NATIVE NORTH AMERICAN CONTEXTUAL MOVEMENT SERIES

Consulting Editor
Corky Alexander

Cherohala Press
Cleveland, Tennessee

INTRODUCTION TO
FIRST NATIONS MINISTRY

CENTRE FOR PENTECOSTAL THEOLOGY
NATIVE NORTH AMERICAN CONTEXTUAL MOVEMENT SERIES

Cheryl Bear-Barnetson

Cherohala Press
Cleveland, Tennessee

Introduction to First Nations Ministry
Centre for Pentecostal Theology Native North American Contextual Movement Series

Published by Cherohala Press, an imprint of CPT Press
900 Walker ST NE
Cleveland, TN 37311
USA
email: cptpress@pentecostaltheology.org
website: www.pentecostaltheology.org

Library of Congress Control Number: 2013948947

ISBN-10: 1935931385

ISBN-13: 9781935931386

All Scriptures quotations are from the New International Version.

Cover design by Laura Zugzda – www.LauraZ.net

Photos by Kevin Clark Photography – www.kevinclarkphotography.com

Original Northwest Coast Artwork by Virgil Dawson

TABLE OF CONTENTS

SERIES PREFACE

The Centre for Pentecostal Theology Native North American Contextual Movement Series celebrates and gives voice to the thought and practices of a growing movement in which Native peoples integrate traditional practices into church life in Pentecostal churches and beyond.

DEDICATION AND ACKNOWLEDGEMENTS

I dedicate this work to my people, the Nadleh Whut'en First Nation from the Carrier Nation located in northern British Columbia. Everywhere I go I introduce myself by where I am from, not what I do, I am Nadleh Whut'en. My family there and the very river and soil of that place have shaped me and made me who I am today. I am related to almost the entire village, and love to visit my two Aunties, Agnes and Irene, and one Uncle, Johnny. I must also mention some of my many cousins there, Kathy, Virginia, Geraldine, and their families. I cannot forget those who have gone on before us. The graveyard is full of people who are still very dear to us and we will always miss them – Uncle Norman George, my cousin Gaylord Sutherland, Grandpa Alec George, and many, many more.

I also acknowledge my remarkable family. My parents are both inspiring people. My Dad, Gottfried (Fred) Schaefer was born in 1936 to Paul and Katerina Schaefer, in what would become East Germany; and as a child, he walked through some of the horrors of the Second World War. He came to Canada in 1958 and later married my Mom, Susie George (now Susan Schaefer) in 1966. She is Nadleh Whut'en from the family of Alec George (Nadleh Whut'en/Cheslatta First Nation) and Martha Camille (Saik'uz First Nation). My mom and our family attended the Lejac Residential School. My brothers Paul and Norman and their families have always been an encouragement to me and I endured difficult times because of their love and well-known sense of humor.

My boys Paul, Randall, and Justice continue to be an inspiration to me. My husband Randy Barnetson is a great evangelist, pastor, and leader, and has been the greatest supporter of my whole life. He has always believed in me and like a true servant-hearted leader, seen things in me that I never knew possible. This project would never have been completed without his love and encouragement. I would like to acknowledge Randy's family as well, all of whom are very dear to me; Randy has three older sons and their families, Aaron & Melissa, Jared & Christianne, and Dan & Shannon, plus we have three wonderful grandchildren, Isaac, Samantha, and Bryce.

My extended family is very important to me – Cindy, Russell, Sandra, Kerry, Bonnie, many nieces and nephews, and their families, and my mother-in-law Joy (who is truly a joy!).

Many Christian sisters and brothers have been very influential in my life, and many indigenous leaders helped me to see how critical it was for me to walk in the dignity of my Elders and to speak on behalf of my people.

Pastor Barry and Carol McGaffin showed love and grace and helped me to begin to articulate theologically my Native worldview. Their wisdom and leadership gave me much to think about and to work on in my life. Their church, Kingsway Foursquare Church in Burnaby, British Columbia, Canada, is where I got my start pastoring because they gave me a chance by becoming a mother-church to our church plant. I will always be grateful to Carol for being such a good example of how to live a strong, faith-filled Christian life.

My life has been influenced by many teachers from Pacific Life Bible College, Regent College, and The King's Seminary: Rob Buzza, Doug and Rebecca Friesen, Dennis Hixson, Grady and Christina Williams, Miriam Adeney, Loren Wilkinson, John G. Stackhouse, Rikk Watts, Bruce Hindmarsh, Thena Ayers, Barbara Mutch, Maxine Hancock, Dr. and Mrs. Chappell, Dr. Wess Pinkham, and Pastor Jack Hayford.

Many more friends and family come to mind who have inspired me because of their example of how to be a strong, indigenous, Christian leader: my mom Susan Schaefer (Carrier), my dad Fred Schaefer, Lizette Hall (Carrier), Mary John (Carrier), Julia and Chuck Lucas (Nuxalk), my Grand Chief Lynda Prince (Carrier), Sophie Thomas (Carrier), Barb and Gerald Casimer (Carrier), Rita Bear-Gray (Cree), Richard and Katherine Twiss (Lakota Sioux), Terry LeBlanc (Micmaq), Bryan Brightcloud (Chiricahua Apache), Jonathan Maracle (Mohawk), Ray Aldred (Cree), Wendy Peterson (Métis), Larry Wilson (Peguis Cree), Adrian Jacobs (Cayuga), Mavis Etienne (Mohawk), Joe (Cree) and Janice McGillis (Stat'xlim), Hector and Linda Hill (Git'xsan), Christina (Nuh-Chal-Nulth) and Virgil Dawson (Carrier; Kwa-kwa-kwa-kwalth), Jeff Yellow Owl (Blackfeet), George and Rita Kallappa (Makaw), Dan and Rita Lundy (Siletz), and Ken and Hannah Pretty-On-Top (Crow).

The culturally diverse cohort I was part of at The King's Seminary was a constant source of encouragement and joy. The continuous welcome by Dr. Wess and the unity and support of the cohort are some of the reasons for my completing the DMin program.

Our people also give great respect to our ancestors who have gone on before us. I acknowledge them here because they are that great cloud of witnesses, and I am here because the prayers they prayed for me during their time on Earth are still being answered today.

LIST OF FIGURES

1

THE NEED FOR AWARENESS

Introduction

This study addresses the drastic need for a measurable increase in awareness of First Nations ministry, worldview, and values.

In response to this problem, the researcher will develop and lead a seminar for Non-Native Pastors and Leaders entitled, *The Introduction to First Nations Ministry*. The seminar will be presented in Foursquare Churches in the United States and Canada.

This Seminar is designed to inform pastors and leaders of the diversity of First Nations ministry with a three-phased approach. The first phase involves a survey which utilizes an ex-post facto diagnostic tool, designed to assess the basic knowledge of pastors and leaders regarding First Nations worldview, values, stereotypes, and religion. Two surveys will assess the pre-exposure and post-exposure mindset of those involved.

The second phase of this project is the 'Introduction to First Nations Seminar' which gives the attendees an opportunity to hear First Nations' worldviews, values, stereotypes, and religion from an indigenous perspective. The material presented relates directly to the survey previously completed by the participants. This project provides relevant material combined with seminar exposure, an indigenous teacher, and a safe place to ask uncomfortable questions.

The final phase examines the post-exposure surveys assessing any increase in awareness (or lack thereof) related to First Nations ministry. Upon completion of the seminar, participants should have a raised awareness of First Nations worldviews, values, stereotypes, and religion.

This project seeks to assist in modifying the perception of the Foursquare Church towards First Nations ministry in Canada and the United States. The Foursquare Church has a proper perspective of First Nations ministry, but there always exists room for deeper understanding and clarity in one's perception of the indigenous People's of Canada and the United States. It is also hoped and anticipated that any Evangelical ministry, church, or denomination will be able to embrace and benefit from this project.

Perspective is a point of view or outlook. Foursquare has seen in the past the usual hang-ups that most denominations have with Native drums and regalia and understands the need for contextualization and for indigenous leadership and churches to be planted. The movement has always striven to foster a good relationship with Native leaders. However, leaders in every denomination have made similar mistakes when working with the First Nations; they assume that if Indians are found in Canada and the United States they must be Canadian and American and fail to recognize the extreme differences in culture.

Perception is about insight, discernments, sensitivity, assessment, and opinion. It can be skewed by many things including ignorance, defined as lack of knowledge or education; distance, living in close proximity to Native people but having no association with them; and politics which can undermine ministry attempts because of presuppositions and misunderstanding. If one does not learn something about the First Nations people, one will continue to live in ignorance and conduct ministry to First Nations people that will continue to be largely ineffective.

Ethnocentrism is 'a belief in or assumption of the superiority of the social or cultural group that a person belongs to'.[1] It is quite normal for one to embrace ethnocentric convictions. North Americans are so familiar with their own culture that they do not even consider it a culture; they believe everything is as it should be.

One can sometimes feel uncomfortable in a new culture. This condition is called 'culture shock', and this perception can vary from mild to extreme. A young person on a mission trip to Mexico suddenly began having an anxiety attack. Her friends told the lead pastor she sometimes had these attacks and asked the pastor to pray for her. Instead of praying, the pastor began to talk to her about where they were and what was occurring. She encouraged the

---

[1] Encarta Dictionary with Microsoft Word 2008.

young person, affirming their proximity to an airport and the avail-
ability of a Visa card in the event of an emergency there or back
home. The young woman immediately calmed down. This incident
was not the result of an evil spirit but rather of culture shock, which
necessitates communication if it is to be overcome.

Another example of culture shock happened in India. An administrative person was asking the pastor leading the team questions
regarding the schedule. However, the pastor could not provide answers because of a slight language barrier and a huge cultural barrier. In India, there is no need for extensive communication. When it
is time to go, one simply follows, however, there is little or no notice of when that might be. The administrative person was asking so
many questions because in Canadian/American culture one asks
questions and receives answers in order to know their place. If
there is free time in the schedule, there is time for shopping, however, if there is an evening meeting planned, there is no personal
time, whereas India is more of a go-with-the-flow type of country.
The administrative type became frantic because he was not able to
plan as he would have liked.

This project will also assist in dealing with any culture shock that
one will most likely experience when ministering to indigenous
people in Canada and the United States. Hopefully, participants will
have an experience so different from their normal life and culture
that the Native people will make an indelible mark on their heart
and soul.

The Setting

The setting of this project is unique to the author's field of study.
She was appointed the Unit Supervisor of the First Nations Unit in
Canada at its inception in 2004 by then President of the Canadian
Foursquare Church, Tim Peterson, and the National Board of
Foursquare Canada. Most Units (known as Districts in the United
States Foursquare Church) are regional, based on a specific prov-
ince or location within a province (e.g. The Coastlands Unit con-
sists of all churches on Vancouver Island in British Columbia). The
First Nations Unit however, is a non-geographical Unit, which
spans the entire country of Canada. The current President of the
Canadian Foursquare Church, Barry Buzza, is working on a Na-

tional Strategy for assimilation starting with the Unit Supervisors. This project will benefit those who seek to further the work started in the heart of God for the First Nations people in Canada.

The United States is included in this project because the history of the indigenous people in the two countries parallel one another. They share the same history of the Residential School (Indian Boarding School) and assimilation attempts by the government.

They also share similar history pertaining to indigenous issues as well as with Foursquare history. Until 1981, Canada itself was a District of the International Church of the Foursquare Gospel. The author also included the United States in this project because she and her family have been living in Los Angeles County for the past three years planting First Nations Churches with her husband Randy and their three boys, Paul, Randall, and Justice, while also attend The King's Seminary.

Pastor Jack W. Hayford, President of The Foursquare Church has a great perspective and perception of First Nations in the United States and Canada. He discussed the need for contextualizing the Gospel for First Nations people several times during the School of Pastoral Nurture (2004-2006), and displayed an immense understanding for and an interest in them.

Former President of the Foursquare Church, Paul Risser, addressed the 2007 Foursquare First Nations District Conference with these words, 'Help the world to see the church as redemptive and not condemning'. This is the goal when initially speaking to Native people about Jesus. Unfortunately, this project will confirm the fact that First Nations people have not always experienced the church as redemptive but rather as condemning. It is the goal of this project to help change the way non-Native pastors and leaders view Native people and thereby facilitate effective ministry and give indigenous people a chance to see the church as it should be, redemptive.

There is also an affinity among First Nations across the two countries based on similar values and culture. Of course there are cultural and linguistic differences between the Coast Salish (British Columbia) and the Mohawk (Ontario), the Chumash (California) and the Maliseet (Maine). They have much more in common with each other than have with their neighboring European Canadian/American friends. This statement is not intended to be discriminatory. Indigenous people have a great affinity with each other and comprise a completely different culture from the dominant culture of Canada and the United States. This theme will resurface throughout this project.

Because the goal of this project is to benefit every Foursquare pastor, it has not been directed to one specific church in a specific city. Within close proximity of every Foursquare Church in The United States and Canada, there is a Reservation (as they are called in the United States) or a Reserve (as they are called in Canada).

Another reason for not allowing the restricting of this project to one specific place is that the author and her family travel. They have journeyed to over 200 Reserves in Canada and Reservations in the United States and have visited almost as many churches, giving a presentation on cultural style worship and talking about ministry to First Nations. Their vision is to assist in equipping Foursquare pastors and leaders in understanding the unique challenges presented to those engaged in First Nations ministry.

The author is an indigenous woman from northern British Columbia, Canada. Her people are commonly known as the Carrier Nation. She is from the Bear Clan and the village of Nadleh Whut'en First Nation. Having been raised in a predominantly White society, yet having a close connection to her people in Nadleh Whut'en, she has personally been a victim of inappropriate missiology. The hope is that this project will affect non-Native pastors' and leaders' conception of and consideration for Native people. Native people also have negative stereotypes of pastors and leaders derived from over 500 years of contact with European missionaries. Missionary methods have only started to change over the last twenty years and hopefully this trend will transform the manner in which this work is conducted among First Nations people in Canada and the United States.

This project is difficult to write because it expresses very candid views associated with the unique problems faced by Native Christians. It is difficult but necessary to present this information in order to honor the indigenous people of the land.

Statement of the Problem

This project addresses the following problem: because non-Native Foursquare pastors and leaders do not always understand the indigenous people originally from Canada and the United States, their ministry can be obstructed and rendered ineffective. The difficult issues presented in this project are the subject of inquiry from anyone dealing with Native people.

In response to this problem, the project will demonstrate that a brief seminar introducing non-Native pastors and leaders to indigenous worldview, stereotypes, values and culture, will greatly increase their comprehension of indigenous peoples and significantly facilitate ministry.

There is sometimes a variance between what one believes and how one performs missiology. One may believe that one should treat people of other nations with respect and apply proper missiology when ministering. However, this often seems only to apply to Nations overseas (and sometimes Mexico), but does not always apply to First Nations.

There are great examples within the Foursquare Churches of Canada and the United States where proper missiology is being directed to the First Nations people and ministry is effective, but there are still examples of pastors and leaders who are trying to work among indigenous people without the necessary basic cross-cultural training. These pastors and leaders perpetuate the negative stereotypes that Native people have of Christians and confirm in the hearts of Native people that they do not want anything to do with Christianity, or 'The White Man's Religion'.

Hypothesis

A measurable increase of awareness of First Nations ministry, worldview, and values will be achieved by non-Native pastors and leaders in a seminar called *The Introduction to First Nations Ministry* given to Foursquare churches in United States and Canada.

Background and Significance

Introduction

'I didn't know Indians could be Christians!' An average American parishioner spoke these words to a friend, a Cahuilla pastor, who had just finished guest preaching at a non-Native church.

'I didn't know Indians could be intelligent.' This comment startled another friend, a Cree pastor who was a guest speaker at a non-Native church in Canada. These statements were not uttered in the 1800's, but within the last few years.[2] Members of Evangelical churches made these statements. It should be obvious that First Nations leaders have many barriers to overcome as they navigate within the church culture of the dominant society.

These striking misunderstandings exemplify the need to teach Christians about indigenous people in Canada and the United States. Of course, these are not quotes from pastors and leaders, but where do people get their ideas? Can churches unwittingly perpetuate these myths? Perhaps Churches are silent about Native issues. To be silent about any issue is to have chosen a side. To be silent about indigenous ministry and the need to promote understanding in Foursquare Churches is to allow misunderstanding, stereotypes, and prejudice to reign.

During the Canadian Foursquare convention in Ottawa a few years ago, the pastors took a tour of the Parliament buildings. Standing at a monument dedicated to women in 1929 they read a plaque, 'We are People'. Women had fought hard to win the right to vote that year.

The author asked the pastors, 'When will they construct the monument to First Nations?' and received some puzzled looks. 'Apparently, before 1960, First Nations were not people. That is when they were given the right to vote in Canada.'

Indigenous people are not overly interested in a monument to commemorate their ability to vote in elections but would much more appreciate understanding, friendship, justice, and reconciliation.

There is a great need in Canada and the United States of America for the healing of the First Nations. There is much misunder-

---

[2] This project was completed in 2008.

standing among non-Native pastors, church leaders, Bible teachers, and denominational leaders about Native people and Native ministry. Many view First Nations as pitiful, a quick and easy mission field, or overlook them altogether. Some pastors and leaders have a great desire to reach out to First Nations but do not know where to start.

Many non-Native pastors and leaders have legitimate questions and issues concerning Native people but feel they cannot inquire because they do not want to appear prejudiced. Many times the questions are prejudicial in nature but come from a good heart that is uninformed and desiring insight. Other questions are completely inappropriate and offensive – but how does one ever determine that a question is discourteous or wounding unless they first ask? This project seeks to create a safe place to explore these issues. If these questions remain unasked and unanswered, the myths, stereotypes and misunderstanding will not only continue, but will proliferate.

There are many metaphors used to describe the Foursquare Church in both Canada and the United States, but the author's favorite is family. It has been said of its founder, Aimee Semple McPherson, that when listening to her sermons it felt as though one was sitting in a room having a conversation, although there were a thousand people in the room. The conversation initiated by this project may not be as comfortable as that room, but this is family and members need to discuss indigenous issues.

Authenticity

Jacquelyn Stewart is a respected elder from Crow Agency, Montana in the Crow Nation. When asked[3] to talk about Crow values, she said that when Crows greet one another they must speak in their language, and if they do not they are not being genuine. To speak and to answer in the Crow language means one is a real person – honest, unbiased, and can be trusted because one is being who one really is. Jacquelyn said that being called a 'real person' is the highest honor one can receive. This value ranks above another strong Native value, respect. To be a 'real' person is a value cherished and expected from others and needs to be inclusively extended.

---

[3] Interviewed by the author in Los Angeles 2006.

Authenticity is valued highly among Christians. What does it mean to be an authentic Christian or live one's life authentically before God. When believers think about living an authentic Christian life, they generally categorize it under spirituality, spiritual exercises, or evangelism. They may believe it only concerns how much they pray, read the Bible; or how often they witness to their unsaved neighbors and friends. That excludes all the other cultural activities in which one engages, such as watching a game or going shopping.

This compartmentalization is not healthy. Living authentically before God means every part of one's life is affected by one's faith: the type of movies/TV shows one watches, the games one plays, the books one reads, how one uses or wastes time, how one treats their children, how one treats a spouse, where (and on what) one spends money and how one treats every person who enters their life.

It means that every aspect of life is lived before God and dedicated to Him. This does not mean that God would frown on one watching a game or going shopping but it does mean that one must conscientiously steward one's life.

Jesus must be fully incarnated into the indigenous culture in order for a First Nations person to be an authentic indigenous Christian. If Christianity cannot relate to who one is as an indigenous person, then it is not true Christianity. When a people group gives up their identity in order to become Christians, they become a grotesque caricature of that nation which is not something Creator intended.

First Nations people today learn from a young age that they are different. They hear racial slurs, prejudice, and see non-Native people react when they enter a room. At home, indigenous youth are taught to be proud of their unique and beautiful culture, but too often Canadian and American society does not value indigenous people. Because of stereotypes and misunderstanding, Native people feel unwelcome and it makes life difficult. Home on the Reserve is a lot different from anywhere else in Canada and United States, everywhere they go is a cross-cultural experience.

The following quote, which comes from a Lakota Catholic Sister, illustrates the need for healing, part of which comes from being honest about the injustices of the past.

It is critically necessary to reflect upon what has happened to us, not only in the Catholic Church, but in Western history. Not to do this would be to deny our very selves and our memory. It would in effect make us hollow people with no identity. If we do not look at both the life and death aspects of our history, we will deprive ourselves of a means for coming to terms with it and of being healed from the psychological wounds it has left within us.

We must admit that our history, in general, has been wiped out of the public memory of the United States of America. We as a people have been trivialized or romanticized out of the conscious memory of most North American people. We must look carefully and long at what this has done to us, especially to our deep inner selves where the image of self is formed and where self-love/self-respect or hatred of self begins. Only after this will we be able to act out of a clear place within us.[4]

Healing for the First Nations begins with Creator. This healing can only be realized when Native people candidly face the past injustices without shame, recognizing their differences with others and moving forward with a sense of forgiveness in order to receive restitution.

Non-Native people can help in this process by being willing to learn and walk alongside of Native people in the midst of their grief and healing. The ancient wounds took a long time to create and they cannot be healed overnight. This process will require years unless the Creator can bring a miracle of healing. Perhaps that miracle will come through understanding non-Native brothers and sisters who come alongside for a journey of healing and true reconciliation.

In the past few years, there has been a movement of reconciliation between Native and non-Native Christians church groups. A non-Native leader and an indigenous leader stand on the platform, they both ask for forgiveness for the injustices of the past in front of a conference or church and alas – it is finished, or not.

The heart intention of these services is well meant but the result is certainly not reconciliation, '... find the next move of God', – is

---

[4] James Treat (ed.), *Native and Christian: Indigenous Voices on Religious Identity in the United States and Canada* (New York: Routledge, 1996), p. 133.

more the result, but there can be no reconciliation without restitution. If non-Native people feel genuine remorse for past injustices, they must help to do something about it besides apologizing. Suppose a man bumps into another man, knocking him into a river. Does he apologize and then walk away leaving the other man in the river? Manners dictate that he would reach out to the other, pulling him to safety, getting him dried off, and then safely on his way. Heartfelt apologies come with a strong desire to make wrong things right. This has simply not been the response within the church at large towards indigenous people.

Values
Values illustrate major differences between non-Native and Native people. Respect is a strong value among indigenous groups, which the elders teach Traditional indigenous people at a young age. The teachings include respect for the beliefs of others and acceptance of people from other cultures. Even if the Traditional does not agree with non-Native ways, they will show respect and simply withdraw. It is only through respect that anyone can gain entrance to begin to be an agent of healing for First Nations people.

Indigenous people value relationships over time. Promptness is not a priority because the relationship takes precedence. Silence is also a value of native people and often they are considered slow or stupid because they do not readily answer a question. If a Native person takes a long time to respond during a discussion, it is because they are showing that they have listened carefully and value one's words. Native people often pause in the middle of their dialogue, not because they are finished but because they are carefully considering their next sentence. This is the best method of discussion and the reason why indigenous people tend to be great orators. Some non-Native speakers believe many words equate to wisdom, while Native people choose words wisely and speak slowly so that every word is heard and understood. During the funeral of an elder there were a number of speeches given to honor the deceased and his family. Near the end of the sharing time a local pastor got up and said, 'You are all so eloquent'. He recognized that after listening to more than fifteen random Native speakers, they were all eloquent.

The most misunderstood value of Native people is the recognition of leadership. Canadian and American leadership values are very different in that individuals who take initiative are admired. Indigenous people differ not because they are unable to take the initiative, but they wait to be recognized. If, in a meeting, someone calls out, 'Someone open in prayer', the non-Native values the person who takes initiative and demonstrates great leadership qualities, whereas, in that setting an indigenous leader would be viewed as not being capable or even as being non-participatory. The Native leader will not step forward because the Native value is to wait and be recognized. Now, which is better? Which value is more godly? They are both acceptable but illustrate how differing values can leave indigenous leaders isolated and ignored for promotion because they do not fit the dominant culture leadership criterion.

Indigenous people place a high value on Elders. The symbol for wisdom is a circle of Elders. That is why one of the descriptive names for Creator is Grandfather. It is not that prayer is directed to ancestors but rather it is assigning Creator a description similar to Ancient One. Indigenous Elders are rarely, if ever, found in a home for the aged. They are cared for in their own home and die in their own beds surrounded by family.

Another indigenous value is not to be proud. Pride evidenced by arrogance and conceit is usually unacceptable in any culture. Being proud of a son's football team, of a Veteran, or being proud of oneself for a difficult accomplishment is good and right. However, the issue here is arrogance and conceit.

Some cultures allow pride even when it is not the good and right type. But in Native culture, no one can get away with being proud. To deal with pride one uses laughter and humor. Native humor is quite surprising because it comes from out of nowhere and is so funny. All Native people have a great sense of humor and love to laugh. It is usually surprising to others who may have preconceived ideas about Native people being stoic or worse, not so smart. However, humor is a large and significant part of Native life.

History

History must be addressed from an indigenous perspective. Most people believe that indigenous history began when Columbus landed. However, Native people go back further than 'discovery'. Native people have oral history and tradition, which includes stories that do not always make sense to the western mind, but are as much a part of our Native people as the land where Creator placed us. Although most discount oral history and tradition because they claim it is unreliable, Christians should know better. The Pentateuch and two of the Gospels are based on oral history and Christians implicitly believe them. Native people have a place in history but some have forgotten or overlooked the Native narrative regarding history. Richard Twiss talks about history as we know it:

> It is said that those who win the wars get to write the history books. Most recorded history is actually a very subjective accounting of past events. People with pen and paper sit down and attempt to accurately and ethically describe their perceptions of events they have seen, heard about and researched – a far cry from any guarantee of accuracy.[5]

Many people falsely believe that American and Canadian indigenous people were 'the bad guys', disturbing the progress and settling of the land. However, from an indigenous point of view, it was not the Indians who were doing the disturbing but rather reacting to being disturbed.

> Historical images infuse the public landscape of the city of Williams Lake in the Central Interior of British Columbia. Downtown streets are named after early settlers and politicians who were prominent in local and provincial life in the 1920's … Similar constructions of history can be found in virtually any small city and town across Canada. Histories commemorating the arrival of early non-Native explorers, settlers, missionaries, and industries in the remote regions of Canada constitute the vast narratives of Canadian nationalism. These narratives comprise what the Marxist literary critic Raymond Williams calls a society's 'selective tradition,' a partial vision of history that provides the official story of that society's past – a story that is produced and communicated in the most significant of public domains, ranging from public schools and national museums to ceremonies of the state, and a story that plays a vital role in rationalizing past

---

[5] Richard Twiss (Lakota Sioux), *One Church many Tribes: Following Jesus the Way God Made You* (Ventura, CA: Regal Books, 2000), p. 37.

and present social institutions and structures of political authority.[6]

In regard to church history among Native people, there have
been many attempts to evangelize them, some good, many not. Today there are many wonderful Native ministries led by indigenous
people who seek to make the gospel relevant to their own people.
Historically, this was not always so, mostly because of the pre-
conceived perception of non-Native people who brought the gospel as equivalent to conquest.

Christopher Columbus was Lost

Going further back into history, Christopher Columbus, a national
hero in the United States is celebrated with his own holiday. Indigenous people were misnamed 'Indians' because until his dying day,
Columbus thought he had discovered India. Indigenous people
were questioning their being misnamed as far back in 1646 when,
'… an unnamed tribesman asked the Massachusetts missionary
John Eliot: "Why do you call us Indians?"'[7]

Sister Archambault (Hunkpapa Lakota) reflects on the Native
response to Columbus Day stating that it should be celebrated as a
victory of survival. She explains that this fabled conqueror is no
hero to Native people:

> After Columbus 'discovered' America, he brought back news of
> a great new world which he assumed to be India and, therefore,
> filled with Indians. Almost at once European folklore devised a
> complete explanation of the new land and its inhabitants which
> featured the fountain of youth, the seven cities of gold, and oth-
> er exotic attractions. The absence of elephants apparently did
> not tip off the explorers that they weren't in India.[8]

Not only is Columbus credited with discovering a place people
had already occupied the land for centuries; he also is credited with
bringing the gospel to the Americas. Many assume Jesus stepped

---

[6] Elizabeth Furniss, 'Pioneers, Progress, and the Myth of the Frontier: The
Landscape of Public History in Rural British Columbia', *BC Studies* 115/116 (Au-
tumn/Winter 1997/98), p. 7.

[7] Robert F Berkhofer Jr., *The White Man's Indian: Images of the American Indian
from Columbus to the Present* (New York: Vintage Books, 1979), p. 4.

[8] Treat (ed.), *Native and Christian*, p. 133.

off the Santa Maria *just after* Columbus. Unfortunately, his perception of the indigenous people gave Europe material to create a plethora of indigenous stereotypes; everything from the raging savage to the simple primitive.

Columbus resolved that Native people would be good subjects and would easily convert to Christianity. He wrote in his log, 'They ought to make good and skilled servants, for they repeat very quickly whatever we say to them. I think they can easily be made Christians, for they seem to have no religion.'[9] From the very beginning of their contact with Europeans, Native people have been subjected to inequality, objectified,[10] and demeaned, how easy then it was for this misinformation to pass through generations until today when average Americans and Canadians have no accurate perception idea about Native peoples.

The Native religion, societal rules, and community are bound together. There is no departmentalization and if one is out of order, the rest are out of order. When the newcomers deemed indigenous culture primitive, their spirituality non-existent (or at the very least deficient), and their manners child-like, they began what would become (to them) a tolerable, systemic attitude of racism, condescension, and subjugation of Native people starting with the very identity of the indigenous person. Not much has changed today politically, socio-economically, and spiritually. Native people are still treated with a degree of disdain. Many people within the walls of our churches base their attitudes towards Native peoples on stereotype and assumption.

Residential Schools – Indian Boarding Schools

The Indian Boarding Schools (United States) and Residential Schools (Canada) were introduced to civilize the savages. The children were taken from their homes, punished for speaking their language, and taught a Euro-American worldview while Christianity was forced upon them. Residential schools are the reason many indigenous people refuse to embrace the gospel of Jesus today. How can we believe in the White Man's God? That remains the question

---

[9] Robert H. Fuson (ed. and trans.), *The Log of Christopher Columbus* (Camden, ME: International Marine Publishing Company, 1987), pp. 77, 80.

[10] *Objectify*: reduce to object; to reduce somebody, or something that is complex and multifaceted, to the status of a simple object. Microsoft Encarta 2008.

today. Many Native people believe that if one becomes a Christian they are turning away from being an Indian and turning white. They accurately base their reasoning on the reality of assimilation efforts exerted by church and state, bound together in an unholy war against Indian children.

> Also undercutting federal aims were conflicting perceptions among Indians and non-Indians of the larger meaning of assimilation and identity. From the vantage point of white America and as articulated through national Indian policies, these were related if not interchangeable concepts. Accomplishment of the first, it was assumed, would produce a corresponding transformation in the second. Complete assimilation – usually termed 'civilization' – would render Indians indistinguishable from whites, facilitate their absorption into the broader American social fabric, and effect a fundamental change of identity in which the images Indians held of themselves as Indians would fade and eventually disappear. Assimilation would be fully realized when Indians ceased to exist, both in mind and being.[11]

In a speech of the Parliamentary Prayer Breakfast attended by a group of indigenous Christians, John McKay, a Minister of Parliament in Canada stated, 'These (indigenous) people are Christians, and we need to ask them "Why are you a Christian?" because we've given them no reason at all to become Christians'.[12]

It certainly is difficult for indigenous people to believe in Jesus because of the unhealed wounds inflicted through these schools. The memory of these days is not that removed in history. Christians must acknowledge that the Residential School brought unprecedented pain and heartache and almost succeeded in destroying the indigenous people, which sadly was the point.

However, the reason indigenous people can become Christians is because Jesus is older than their contact with the white man. Jesus is an ancient tribal man whose people also struggled under a dominant culture. In general, Christians are unable to discern their

---

[11] Cary C. Collins, 'Editor's Introduction', in Edwin L. Chalcraft, *Assimilation's Agent: My Life as a Superintendent in the Indian Boarding School System* (ed. Cary C. Collins; Lincoln, NE: University of Nebraska, 2004), p. xviii.

[12] May 2, 2007, The Evangelical Fellowship of Canada's Aboriginal Council was invited to this Prayer Breakfast on Capitol Hill, Ottawa, Ontario, Canada.

own entrenched position because, as a part of the dominant culture, they are blinded by their own dominance.

The government administered these schools but most often priests and nuns, from several different denominations, conducted daily operations. However, the founder of these schools, a military man named Richard Pratt, had the motto, 'Kill the Indian, save the man'.

> The nineteenth-century slogan devised by R.H. Pratt, the founder of Carlisle Indian School, summed it up nicely: 'Kill the Indian … and save the man.' Since 'kill the Indian' was a clear metaphoric reference to Indian culture and values – specifically religious values and cultural practices – the slogan affirmed what was the latest effort to force the social and cultural transformation of Indian persons, particularly children from Indian into euro-American clones.[13]

Pratt, the father of the Residential Schools (he used to call himself father to the children under his supervision), saw indigenous people as a problem to be remedied.

> (Pratt's) plan preached emancipation, the liberation of Indian children from the retarding influences of their parents, families, and tribes through their placement in large boarding schools located far from reservations. In such a benign setting, in an environment unencumbered by outside interference, students could become fully immersed in white America. In 1879, Pratt and another army officer, Melville C. Wilkinson, convinced the federal government of the merits of this approach, which in turn approved funding for two off-reservation boarding schools, one on each coast. Carlisle in Pennsylvania and Chemawa in Oregon. Over the next two decades dozens of such 'total' institutions were built.[14]

Before the Residential Schools were founded, Canada was already passing legislation that would assimilate the indigenous people. In 1857, Canada passed the Gradual Civilization Act. 'Its premise was that by eventually removing all legal distinctions between

---

[13] George E. Tinker, *Spirit and Resistance: Political Theology and American Indian Liberation* (Minneapolis: Fortress Press, 2004), p. 38.

[14] Collins, 'Editor's Introduction', p. xxi.

Indians and non-Indians through the process of enfranchisement, it would be possible in time to absorb Indian people fully into colonial society.'[15] Subsequently, from 1870 to 1910, the government of Canada and missionaries from various denominations began the process of assimilating indigenous people into Canadian society. By 1920, children between the ages of seven and twelve were forced by police officers, priests, and Indian agents to attend the Residential Schools. In 1931, there were eighty schools in operation. By 1948, there were seventy-two schools with 9,368 students.[16] In the 1980's stories began to surface about sexual and physical abuse suffered in Residential Schools. The Assembly of First Nations began to look into these issues and in 1998 they established the Indian Residential Schools Resolution Unit.

The Residential Schools were houses of assimilation. The government wanted to deal with the Indian problem and did so by giving grants to those, such as Pratt in Pennsylvania, who started the first-ever Indian boarding school in Carlisle, and Chalcraft for a school in Chemawa, Oregon. They fully believed they were doing indigenous people a service by teaching them not only schoolwork, but also by forcing a non-indigenous worldview upon mere children. Some ex-boarding school students from Britain (now Canadian or American) claim that they suffered under the British boarding school system and are now doing well. They say horrible things such as, 'We survived and do not whine about our traumatic experiences so you Indians should just get over it already!'[17] The difference between experiences however, is severe.

It would be radically different if Indian children were placed in boarding schools where their indigenous language was spoken, where the teachers were from the same nation as the children and shared worldview, and culture. Certainly, this was the circumstance under which British schoolchildren attended boarding schools *in Britain*; however, this was not the situation in Canada and the United States.

---

[15] From Indian and Northern Affairs Canada website: http://www.ainc-inac.gc.ca/ch/rcap/sg/sg23_e.html

[16] From Indian and Northern Affairs Canada website: http://www.ainc-inac.gc.ca/ch/rcap/sg/sg23_e.html

[17] The author has heard this spoken by Christians, more than a few times.

The only hypothetical comparison that can articulate the extreme difference of the British Boarding school to the Residential Schools (in Canada and the United States) is if American schoolchildren, forcibly taken out of their Christian homes, were placed in Muslim schools to learn a new language, religion, and culture or endure corporal punishment.[18]

That analogy is quite shocking and no offense is meant to Muslims but to drive home a point that these schools were totally and completely different, and in reality, a cruel step into a confusing and punishing new world. The following quote is from a song that describes the first mother and son ever separated by the boarding schools.

My son when they took you away,
    you were so young and strong

I just couldn't wait for the day to have you
    back home where you belong

The only thing that kept me alive,
    was knowin' I would see you again

There was no way for me to know,
    you'd come back a man I don't know

My son, where did you go when they took you away?

I don't recognize you anymore,
    the scars of life are deeper than before

No, I don't recognize you anymore

Mother when I went away,
    I looked back to my home

You know I really wanted to stay
    when I thought of you there all alone

The only thing that kept me alive,
    was knowin' I would see you again

---

[18] The hypothetical situation is not meant to offend any religion, whether Christian or Muslim, but rather to drive home a point of the vast diversity of culture, language, and worldview between Indigenous students in Canada and the United States and the British styled boarding schools.

There was no way for me to know,
    I'd come back to an alcoholic home.

Mother, where did you go when they took you away?

I don't recognize you anymore,
    the scars of life are deeper than before

No, I don't recognize you anymore.[19]

After hearing this song, a respected elder[20] in the community of Lillooet wrote about her childhood boarding school experiences. She said that arriving home for Christmas holidays was the first time she ever witnessed her mother passing out drunk. Never before had her mother drunk until the children were taken away to boarding school.

Many of the parents knew that the years to come would bring many more immigrants and they wanted their children to learn, excel, and not be left behind so they allowed their children to be taken. They did this however by means of selective adaptation.[21] Native people have always believed and continue to believe that certain non-Native ways can be adopted and utilized for the betterment of their communities. However, they did not always agree to relinquish entirely their culture.

The severe results shattered the soul of the Native communities. What began in the heart of Richard Pratt spread across the United States and Canada. The schools were based on strict regimen because Pratt's only preparation for teaching was a stint in the army.

Stories from an Elder

Lizette Hall attended Lejac Residential School for the Dakelh people near Fraser Lake, British Columbia, Canada. The following details some of her experiences: 'Unfamiliar rules were made. There was to be no communications verbal or otherwise between the boys

---

[19] From Indian and Northern Affairs Canada website: http://www.ainc-inac.gc.ca/ch/rcap/sg/sg23_e.html

[20] Winter 2008.

[21] Collins, 'Editor's Introduction', pp. xx-xxi.

and girls. Native languages were forbidden. English was the only allowable language.'[22]

Once she ran away to attend a dance and was brought back to the school. The priest struck her hands eight times each with a willow stick. They were so swollen she could not hold a pencil for a week.[23]

'In the seventies, I mentioned all these injustices to George Clutesi, punishments, etc. He said to me, "You think you were the only ones who had it bad, we had the same treatments in the Anglican Church schools".'[24] Although Lizette confided in someone, nothing was done. Perhaps George Clutesi did have a difficult time in the Anglican Church boarding schools, but it was nothing compared to the cultural genocide afflicted upon indigenous students through the Indian boarding schools via the government and the church. The Anglican students were the same culture, language, and ethnicity of those operating the schools. The experiences of the indigenous children are indescribably more shocking.

> I remember vividly the case of the twelve year old boy from Stoney Creek. His name was Evan. He was a very gentle person and related to my mother. One morning mother came visiting me. She and I were walking past the kitchen. The boys' yard was on the east side of the building and fenced in. We saw Evan some distance from the fence. He was bent over, with hands over his chest and appeared to be in pain. Mother called out to him and asked him what the problem was, between sobs Evan said, 'Father Allard poked me with a cue' pointing to his diaphragm. There was not much mother could do and she went home. Three weeks later we heard Evan died. He is buried at the Mission cemetery.[25]

These tragedies are some of the worst to describe because these events happened in the early 1900's – not that long ago. The author met Lizette Hall and talked with her about these circumstances and specific incidents. Lizette knew and thought very highly of Alec

---

[22] Lizzette Hall (Carrier), *The Carrier, My People* (Cloverdale, BC: Friesen Printers, 1992), p. 81.

[23] Hall (Carrier), *The Carrier, My People*, p. 82.

[24] Hall (Carrier), *The Carrier, My People*, p. 81.

[25] Hall (Carrier), *The Carrier, My People*, p. 83.

George, the author's grandfather who also attended school at the same time. These events did not happen in the 'old west' or to some unknown relative. They occurred only two generations ago and their descendents continue to face the consequences of the policies of these schools today.

The following is a common story for Residential School. Many times the parents were never notified if their child was hurt or died.

> I also recall the five-year-old boy from Shelley. He came to school in the fall of, if I remember correctly 1919. Every one loved him because he was such a happy little fellow. For some reason or another he died either in October or November. We did not hear what he died of … Anyway, my mother came to visit us between Christmas and New Year. She was accompanied by Betsy Gagne of Shelley. Betsy was in tears, crying broken-heartedly. So I asked mother why this woman was crying. Apparently Betsy had come to visit her little boy and was told he had died in the Falltime (sic). Nobody notified her of her child's death.[26]

This is the one of the most vivid and terrible stories regarding the Residential School/boarding school; 'One winter in the thirties, five boys ran away from Lejac school. They tried to walk home on the ice to Fort Fraser. A blizzard came up. After searching, they were found frozen to death, huddled together.'[27]

What horrors would cause these boys to run away on such a cold day in the winter? They were children in the early 1900's, not like children today who have no knowledge of how to survive in the winter. They would have been taught the dangers of the cold winters.[28]

---

[26] Hall (Carrier), *The Carrier, My People*, p. 83.

[27] Hall (Carrier), *The Carrier, My People*, p. 83. The author's Auntie, Agnes Sutherland, said these boys were Nadleh Whut'en, from our Reserve.

[28] The author's grandfather, Alec George, was around the same age as these boys and Lizette knew him from school. He had a tremendous respect for nature and knew much about trapping and hunting. He taught his boys many things. Therefore the Lejac school boys certainly knew the dangers they faced by running away in the winter yet they braved the cold instead of staying at the school.

In March 2001, some 7,200 former Residential School students[29] filed a class action suit against Canada. They desired retribution for the harms received during their attendance at these schools and by 2007 they had won a judgment and payments began to be distributed.[30] However, what amount of money can compensate for such humiliation and tragedy? No amount could ever be enough to make restitution for what the children suffered and indigenous people continue to suffer through the great fragmentation of indigenous society.

Christians who desire to undertake ministry to indigenous people in Canada and the United States must be honest about their part in these schools. There is a continued ongoing pressure that everyone should be the same (in both countries). However, ministry cannot be accomplished unless the minister is able to recognize and honor the vast differences between Euro-Canadians/Americans and indigenous people.

Edwin Chalcraft was a superintendent in the boarding school Chemawa located in western Washington. He was a good friend of Richard Pratt[31] and fully believed that Indian Boarding schools were the only means of helping Native people.

> … Chalcraft recognized the problems common to off-reservation Indian schools. He knew students often suffered from culture shock, family separation, overcrowding, antiquated facilities, unappetizing and inadequate food, poor sanitation, and deficient health supervision, among others. And as superintendent he enforced the institution's emphasis on regimentations, student labor, and discipline. Nonetheless, Chalcraft perceived Chemawa above all as an opportunity, a singular chance, the one hope for Indian people to improve upon what he regarded as their otherwise sorry lot in life.[32]

There is no way to measure the devastating effects the Residential/Indian Boarding schools have had on First Nations in Canada and the United States. Some attribute the soaring rates of suicide

---

[29] '7,200 students filed suit': http://www.cstc.bc.ca/cstc/82/residential+schools.

[30] For more information see: http://www.residentialschoolsettle-ment.ca.

[31] Collins, 'Editor's Introduction', pp. xxi-xxii.

[32] Collins, 'Editor's Introduction', p. iii.

among the youth and the high alcohol and drug abuse rates, directly to the loss of self-esteem that resulted directly from the implementation of the culturally genocidal plan of these schools. No doubt, even a simple overview of the history of these schools is enough to sound a mournful note in any heart.

Conclusion to Background and Significance

How does one interact with someone who is different? How does one befriend someone who talks, thinks, and acts contrary to what one understands as 'normal social behavior'? Does one smooth over these differences, stating, 'God is color blind' or can people be painfully honest with each other and recognize that each person was created differently? God is not colorblind, our Creator invented color, distinctiveness, and diversity.

Desired Results

The goal of this project is to enable non-Native Foursquare pastors and leaders to achieve a greater understanding of indigenous people of Canada and the United States, so that effective ministry can take place and Native people can experience the healing from the Great Spirit of Ancient Wounds. For too long, negative stereotypes and assumptions have dominated the thinking of non-Native leaders across Canada and the United States. If these two countries are serious about reaching indigenous people for Christ, thought processes and resultant actions must be transformed.

Walking alongside the larger body of Christ in unity does not mean uniformity. Indigenous people deserve the right to self-theologize and to have autonomy over their churches. In order to be an authentic expression of the Church, indigenous people must utilize indigenous methods of teaching, learning, establishing bible schools, raising up leaders, licensing and ordination, ceremony, church style and much more. It is also the hope of this project that Christian indigenous people will be given a voice within the church.

Definition of Terms

Aboriginal

A term referring to 'the first to inhabit a region'.[33] This designation will not be used in this project because of the connotation that indigenous people merely arrived on this land first, thereby diminishing their stories, values, and teachings. Their stories state that Creator placed them here. The first rule of any anthropologist worth his or her salt is to listen to the people and not make quick judgments. If this rule is not adhered to, one will not gain people's trust or make any progress in attempting to understand their culture and worldview. So take a deep breath and get ready to dive into some unfamiliar and hopefully not-too-murky water on a journey to raise one's awareness of some of the world's most interesting and beautiful people on planet Earth.

Colonialism

'Taking a bit of the mother country, transplanting it in a foreign place, then promoting and developing it.'[34]

Dichotomy

This term refers to a separation of different or contradictory things; a separation into two divisions that differ widely from or contradict each other.

Ethnocentrism

A term referring to 'a belief in or assumption of the superiority of the social or cultural group that a person belongs to'.[35]

First Nations

A term referring to any indigenous person in Canada and the United States who is part of a people group that has a language, culture, custom, religion and leadership.

Although Métis generally do not prefer to be listed under First Nations, the author considers them as a Nation. References made to First Nations include Alaskan, Nunavut, First Nations, those

---

[33] Anne Waters (ed.), *American Indian Thought: Philosophical Essays* (Oxford, UK: Blackwell Publishing, 2004), p. 82.

[34] Adrian Jacobs (Cayuga: Six Nations), *Aboriginal Christianity: the Way It Was Meant to Be* (Rapid City, SD: Adrian Jacobs, 1998), p. 7.

[35] Encarta Dictionary with Microsoft Word 2008.

who call themselves Aboriginals and other terms. If a people has a language, culture, custom, religion, and leadership they are considered a Nation. This term, therefore, will consistently be used in this project to refer and to honor all of the above.

Indian

This term was given to the indigenous people of North American by explorers from Europe. It has both positive and negative connotations for the indigenous people here today. It evokes favorable implications because some believe Columbus meant *Indios*, Spanish meaning, '*In God*'. This viewpoint asserts that Christopher Columbus' initial impression was that the indigenous people were as Creator made them, untouched by common European sins such as greed and materialism. The term *Indian* also has negative connotations because many believe Columbus misnamed First Nations people. He was lost and until his dying day believed that he had discovered India, oddly without the spices. This term has fallen out of use in an attempt at political correctness. However, if *Indian* is used in this project it will be with the thought that the original inhabitants of North America were *in Dios*.

Indigenous

'Belonging to a place; originating in and naturally living, growing, or occurring in a region or country; natural or inborn.'[36] This term often will be used because it is in the stories of the people of the land which Creator placed them and asked them to care for and of which they were to be good stewards.

Native American

This designation is commonly used in the United States to refer to a person who is from one of the Nations that lived here prior to contact with Europeans. It is a term that can be used in both North and South America because of the indigenous people who inhabit the Americas.

---

[36] Encarta Dictionary with Microsoft Word 2008.

Native

'Born or originating in a particular place; relating or belonging to somebody or something because of the place or circumstances of birth.'[37]

It is used in this study because it is the name with which the author grew up. It simply means Native to the soil that is now North America. It can refer (unfortunately in some cases for indigenous people worldwide) to flora and fauna, i.e. Arizona's only indigenous palm tree is known as *Washingtonia Arizonica*. There are far more palm trees that have been planted in Arizona, but there is only one that is indigenous to the area.

Ontology

Ontology is the most general branch of metaphysics, and is concerned with the nature of being; a particular theory of being.

Primitive

'Relating to or occurring at the first stages or form of something; relating to or appearing in an earlier stage of biological development, particularly of an embryo or species; crudely simple in design or construction (offensive in some contexts).'[38] One could ask a Christian who does not believe in evolution why he or she accepts the statement that indigenous people were primitive? (Note: this is a highly offensive word to First Nations, please never use it).

Regalia

Regalia is traditional indigenous dress. Some wrongly call regalia a Native costume. However, the word costume is offensive because a costume is something one wears when pretending to be someone or something else. Regalia is what indigenous people wear because it represents who they really are. Much of the regalia is handed down from one generation to another and is very precious. Every piece means something. On the North West Coast button blanket, every button sewn represents a person, event, or a prayer.

Reservation/Reserve

Reservation is a term used in the United States meaning an area of land set aside for First Nations people, sometimes the traditional

---

[37] Encarta Dictionary with Microsoft Word 2008.
[38] Encarta Dictionary with Microsoft Word 2008.

land of the indigenous people. Reserve is used in Canada in the same manner as above, however in Canada all Reserves are considered sovereign land of the people who occupy them. In the United States there are other delineations such as Federal and State recognized tribes, but only federally recognized Reservations are considered sovereign Nations within the United States. In Canada, Reserves are most often the original, traditional land of the indigenous people and are referred to as Nations. These terms will be used interchangeably in this project. The term 'Reserve' will never be utilized to mean military (unless duly noted).

Traditional/Traditionals
A term referring to an indigenous person who follows the ways of their ancestors learned through mentoring by Elders.

Medicine Man/Woman
A term referring to one who adheres to practices passed down through traditional knowledge from Elders, which involve healing through herbs and medicines found in nature.

Limitations of Study

Cultural limitations – the first limitation of this project – relates to creating a project. Helping non-native people understand Native people through the use of an academic paper is not something that Native people normally undertake. That type of familiarization more commonly occurs through relationships and community. The best way to minister to Native people is to get to know them within their specific context. However, this project complements many current academic books written by Native leaders to help others understand Native people because most Native academics are extremely upset over being misunderstood and marginalized.

Non-specific overview limitation – Unfortunately this project cannot delve into the intricacies of the more than one thousand different First Nations found in the Unite States and Canada. There are over one thousand distinct Nations (meaning they have languages, culture, customs, religion, and leadership). This project rather will serve as an overview of all indigenous people and their affinity with one another across Canada and the United States.

Indigenous peoples worldwide – Although there are indigenous people in many other countries of the world they are not included in this project. This project specifically deals with the indigenous people living in the United States and Canada because their histories have many similarities and there are First Nations that cross the border of the two countries. There are a number of differences between the two governments dealing with First Nations people; however, there are sufficient similarities to make this a valid study.

There are also First Nations that cross the United States and Mexico border, but they cannot be accommodated in the scope of this project. The indigenous people of Mexico and further south are beautiful and worthy of such a study but, unfortunately, this project will need to be limited to Canada and the United States. The First Nations to the south have many more issues with their governments that are often more serious and discrimination is much more prominent. This project can also bring understanding to help the indigenous people of North, Central, and South America because many similarities are shared with them and with indigenous peoples all over the world.

Canadian and American differences – This project is written from an indigenous perspective and the author is aware that there are substantial differences between the Canadian and American worldviews and cultures: they are very different places. However, the focal point is on the indigenous people who are found within their borders and the consistency and affinity that exists between Native Nations in spite of the border.

Some may believe that one country has treated Native peoples better or worse than the other. The truth is that both countries have implemented both appropriate and inappropriate missiology relating to First Nations people. However, addressing that comparison is not the purpose of this project. The purpose is to raise awareness and take steps to ensure proper ministry is effected for Native people. The author will use American English spelling.

Assumptions

An assumption in this project is that the project will, in fact, assist Foursquare pastors and leaders in Canada and the United States to understand better and, therefore, minister to the First Nations. This will only occur if they sense the need for such a study and recognize that it can benefit the ministries of non-Native pastors and leaders across these lands.

A second assumption is more prophetic in nature. Foursquare, above all other denominations, has the ability to minister grace and healing to First Nations because of its unique style of ministry and a distinctive anointing that God has placed on Foursquare pastors and leaders, especially considering that Foursquare Churches are all indigenous.[39] It is the hope and assumption of this project that Foursquare pastors and leaders will take their place and begin to or in a stronger way continue to minister to the indigenous people of the two countries.

A caution is worthy of mention, however. Vine Deloria Jr. states that Native people do not need white people to understand them. This is truly the case. Most Native people do not appreciate an-thropologists (with a few notable exceptions such as Dr. Miriam Adeney, Regent College, BC, Dr. Doug Pennoyer and Dr. Doug Hayward, Biola, CA and others) because they do not want to be poked, prodded, and are weary of being studied. Why is the author then writing another 'study of Indians'? The reason is to avoid the terrible things that can still transpire in Native ministry because of lack of knowledge. Learning a few details of the indigenous people can promote healing and unity.

'My heart is for my people.'

---

[39] Because all Foursquare Churches are indigenous to their locale, they are rarely a 'fish out of water' but rather always seem to fit into their neighborhood. Few Foursquare churches simply copy the format of another church.

2

FOUNDATIONS OF INDIGENOUS THEOLOGY

Introduction

The purpose of this project is to measure the effectiveness of the Introduction to First Nations Ministry Seminar. The purpose of this chapter is to provide the theological foundation necessary to anticipate and also to introduce certain questions that inevitably surface when discussing First Nations ministry. Indigenous people have an unwritten understanding of Creator passed down through the oral tradition of their ancestors. There are similarities consistent with Christianity. This section will also deal with questions that arise out of stereotypical conceptions of indigenous belief and spirituality.

This section will present indigenous thoughts on Creator, beliefs, and customs. This is an area often misunderstood by non-Native people. Non-Natives sometimes believe that all things indigenous are, at the very least, suspicious and, at the very worst, evil. Native tradition, culture, and custom are not from the devil. The *darkening*[1] has skewed some aspects of indigenous culture, but also has misled all cultures. This is true of certain Native traditional practices as well. Not all traditional practices be 'sanctified' and used in Native churches.

More colleges are inviting First Nations Elders and leaders to speak on indigenous religion, worldview, and beliefs. There is a new respect for indigenous knowledge and people. However, during the

---

[1] The darkening: A time when people stopped worshipping the invisible Creator and exchanged their knowledge of the truth for sinful ways.

author's early days in Bible College, Native Religion was only mentioned in a class called Religions of the World.[2] In 1998, the teacher
showed a picture of a totem pole and declared it an idol. After explaining to the teacher and students that totem poles are not idols,
the author realized that many people, even college teachers, genuinely need help because they do not have the basic facts about
North American indigenous people.

The truth is that all Native tribes held certain beliefs but all embraced a foundational belief in the Creator. As Walking Buffalo,
(Stoney) from Alberta, Canada (1871-1967) puts it,

> We saw the Great Spirit's work in almost everything: sun, moon,
> trees, wind, and mountains. Sometimes we approached Him
> through these things ... we have a true belief in the supreme be-
> ing, a stronger faith than that of most whites who have called us
> pagans ... Indians living close to nature and nature's ruler are
> not living in darkness.[3]

Theology teaches that one cannot 'comprehend the fullness of
God's Nature, nor can we know completely all His plans and designs'.[4] However, the quote above also advises that Creation reveals
its Creator to humankind through, as is said in theological terms,
Natural Theology.[5]

One can know God through Jesus, 'And we know also that the
Son of God has come and has given us understanding, so that we
may know him who is true' (1 Jn 5.20).

Theology is the study of God. To learn about God, Christians
have always turned to the Bible. The Bible is the infallible word of
God. To learn about God, indigenous people have turned to relationships, mannerisms, and cycles found in nature and each other.
Indigenous people have a strong respect for Creator. The quotes
from chiefs in the 19th Century or Elders quoted throughout this
project exemplify this respect, as do the descriptive names and stories of Creator from many nations.

---

[2] Formerly known as Cults 101.

[3] Cited in Michael Oren Fitzgerald, *Indian Spirit* (Bloomington, IN: World
Wisdom, 2003), p. 17.

[4] Fitzgerald, *Indian Spirit*, p. 50.

[5] Guy P. Duffield and N.M. Van Cleave, *Foundations of Pentecostal Theology* (Los
Angeles, L.I.F.E. Bible College, 1987), p. 49.

In order to understand the indigenous perspective, this section of the project includes the theological perspective of God as Creator Great Spirit, Holy Spirit, Water-Fire-Smoke, and the Great Mystery of the Incarnation plus an overview of the Apostle Paul's missionary dealings with a foreign culture.

There are many points of agreement between Christian teachings and indigenous beliefs. The theological community needs to work together with First Nations towards self-theologizing in order for the gospel to be the Good News it was meant to be, productive and constructive rather than disparaging, judgmental, and destructive. Regarding theology, indigenous belief often concurs with the Torah's understanding of God/Creator and with the legalism of purification ceremonies. In fact, this Scripture sounds like a quote from one of the old chiefs, 'The heavens are yours, and yours also the earth; you founded the world and all that is in it' (Ps. 89.11).

The following quote expresses the Christian view of God that aligns with the beliefs of First Nations traditional views: 'Several statements about God in Scripture define various aspects of His Nature, such as: "God is Spirit" (John. 4:24), "God is light" (1 John 1:5), and "God is a consuming fire" (Heb. 12:29).'[6]

God is a spirit means that He cannot be 'confined to a physical body, nor to dimensions of space and time. He is the invisible, Eternal God.'[7]

Christian doctrine states that one knows God by His attributes. God is omnipresent (God is everywhere), omniscient (God knows everything), and omnipotent (God is all-powerful), Immutable (God does not change), self-existent (God was not created), sovereign.[8] Regarding God's moral attributes, Scripture tells us that God is holy, just, righteous, love, merciful, good, and truth.[9]

The works of God also reveal something of His character. God is a Creator and has a divine purpose for the people and for the land.

---

[6] Duffield and Van Cleave, *Foundations of Pentecostal Theology*, p. 56.

[7] Duffield and Van Cleave, *Foundations of Pentecostal Theology*, p. 56.

[8] Duffield and Van Cleave, *Foundations of Pentecostal Theology*, p. 73. 'God can be sovereign without violating Man's essential freedom.'

[9] Duffield and Van Cleave, *Foundations of Pentecostal Theology*, pp. 74-79.

For this is the PURPOSE that is purposed upon the whole earth: and this is the hand that is stretched out upon all nations. For the Lord of hosts hath PURPOSED, and who shall disannul it? And his hand is stretched out, and who shall turn it back? (Isaiah 14:26, 27) (Emphasis from Duffield and Van Cleave)[10]

The evangelical faith emphasizes the teaching of the Trinity and that all are invited into the beauty, love, and community of the Triune God. One cannot penetrate the mystery of the Trinity but it is clear from Scripture that God exists in three persons, and at the same time, as one God. One can read of their presence in the Bible at the baptism of Jesus where the Holy Spirit descends in the form of a dove and a voice from heaven says, 'This is my beloved Son' (Lk. 3.22). Jesus names the three persons of the Trinity when giving instructions on baptism in Mt. 28.19, '... baptizing them in the name of the Father, and of the Son, and of the Holy Ghost'.[11] Another Scripture where the Trinity is found is in the apostolic benediction in 2 Cor. 13.14, 'The grace of the Lord Jesus Christ, and the love of God, and the communion of the Holy Ghost, be with you all. Amen.'[12]

With no differentiation, indigenous people of Canada and the United States understand the essence of the Holy Spirit as being equivalent to the Great Spirit. This is very much like the ancient Hebrew understanding of Yahweh the One God and the continuing understanding the Jewish people have of Yahweh today in disputing the existence of the Triune God. Indigenous people would recognize the Great Spirit as discussed above, however, there are no words or thoughts of a separate being, such as Pneumatology, the Christian theology of the Spirit. The Holy Spirit found in Native beliefs is often mistaken as an energy, essence, or simply presence. When an indigenous person walks through the forest something unique happens, which anyone can experience if one pays attention. The most frequent occurrence for Natives is when they sense something.

In this quote, Fools Crow, Oglala Sioux (1890-1989), uses Christian language to describe Creator:

---

[10] Duffield and Van Cleave, *Foundations of Pentecostal Theology*, p. 56.

[11] Duffield and Van Cleave, *Foundations of Pentecostal Theology*, p. 90.

[12] Duffield and Van Cleave, *Foundations of Pentecostal Theology*, p. 90.

In these six directions is found everything needed for renewal, physical and intellectual growth, and harmony. There is Wakan Tanka himself, God the 'highest and most holy One'; there is Tunkashila, Grandfather; who corresponds to the Son of God; there is Grandmother Earth; and there are the four cardinal directions, moving in order of importance from west to north to east to south. Wakan Tanka is unlimited (infinite), and has given to each of the other directions sacred powers that are their own to impart as they see fit, including such things as purification, joy, good health, growth, endurance, wisdom, inner peace, warmth, and happiness. The directions are holy and mysterious beings. Wakan Tanka remains above them in power and they are not separated even though they are distinct and identifiable. The powers do the will of God, yet they have a will and intellect of their own. They hear and answer prayers, yet their powers and ways remain mysterious. With them and through them we send our voice to God.[13]

For many, after reading this quote, the overwhelming desire is to begin correcting and analyzing these words. However, one should submit to the law of love (and anthropology) that motivate all to walk together towards Creator. Let these words sit in one's heart, meditate, and see where one agrees and can move forward. If one hears words like these coming from indigenous people, the appropriate response should be that of gratitude. If they trust enough to share their thoughts about Creator, welcoming one to journey with them, one can join their journey together towards Creator. The missionary must now take the place of a learner before daring to imagine they have anything to offer indigenous people. Does theology transcend culture or must it come through culture? Dominant cultures do not ask this question because they assume true theology is best expressed through their own culture. However, by observing the manner in which other cultures think and talk about God, one can learn much about God and one's self.

In October 2005, recognized First Nations Elder, Saginaw Grant from the Sax and Fox Nation, opened the Pasadena Powwow with prayer. He said a wonderful prayer full of gratitude. He prayed for the troops, for veterans, and for the poor here at home. It was a

---

[13] Cited by Fitzgerald, *Indian Spirit*, p. 50.

solemn moment for all and he led us to the Creator. Mr. Grant would not describe himself as a Christian, he is a Traditional and like many other Traditional indigenous people, he believes strongly in the Creator. Every First Nations gathering across Canada and the United States opens with prayer to the Creator. Indigenous people always acknowledge and have great respect for the Creator. The attributes of the Creator are similar to the attributes of the God of the Bible and First Nations' cleansing ceremonies resemble the purification ceremonies of the Torah.

The theology section of this project seeks to answer questions raised in the seminar by non-Native pastors and leaders. These non-Native leaders were genuinely interested in walking alongside indigenous people on a journey to Creator but were also very concerned that indigenous people have an appreciation for proper theology. Interestingly, an indigenous person would not want to label their belief as a 'study' or 'doctrine', but would rather equate their belief to a spiritual journey that cannot be explained by a book.

Indigenous people believe that everyone is on a journey to Creator but some get lost along the way, caught up in the selfishness of life, or distracted by worries or greed.

The Creator Great Spirit – Doctrine 101

A question that burns in the mind of every non-Native Christian when thinking about Indians: 'Is Indian religion evil?' That is a valid question for American or Canadian people to ask, however it is very offensive for a Native person to hear. Please do not think that indigenous people are overly sensitive, they are not. After five hundred years of being scrutinized, stereotyped, and misunderstood, indigenous people often feel overly exposed. Christians react in a similar fashion when radical Islamists state that Christianity is a false, polytheistic religion.

However, and rightly so, many feel a number of questions deserve to be answered in order for there to exist the community God intended for all His children. It is the goal of this project to provide many of these answers and to open a dialogue between non-Native and Native Christian leaders.

Theology teaches that one cannot 'comprehend the fullness of God's Nature, nor can we know completely all His plans and designs'.[14] First Nations have often seen The Great Mystery in creation and have been labeled animists,[15] monists,[16] polytheists,[17] or pantheists.[18] The author does not believe that the indigenous ancestors fit these classifications. Indigenous people are not animists simply because they regard animals, who share breath with humans, as brothers or relatives. They simply have a great respect for nature and all life. Indigenous knowledge means that Creator is watching with great attentiveness and love for all creation and therefore respect is due.

Whenever a Native person kills an animal (never for sport), they will always thank the animal for giving their life to feed the hunter's family. One life is given so that the hunter can feed his family; he or she then out of respect, acknowledges the life that was given while

---

[14] Duffield and Van Cleave, *Foundations of Pentecostal Theology*, p. 50.

[15] According to Ralph D. Winter and Steven C. Hawthorne (eds.), *Perspectives on the World Christian Movement: A Reader* (Pasadena: William Carey Library, 1992), p. D-108, the term 'animism' has fallen out of usage *except* when questioning indigenous spirituality:

> The popular use of the term Animism comes down to us from E.B. Tylor (1871). He did not give it the technical meaning it acquired from the comparative religionists, of a 'kind of religion,' but used it to signify, 'the deep-lying doctrine of Spirit Beings, which embodies the very essence of Spiritualistic as opposed to Materialistic philosophy.' It was for him a 'minimum definition of religion' which saw the animistic way of life as accepting the reality of spiritual force(s) and being over against the materialistic outlook on life. In its full development, Tylor agreed, it formulated concrete beliefs in such notions as the soul(s), the future state, controlling deities and subordinate spirits, especially when there beliefs result in 'some kind of active worship'.

[16] 'Substantival monism ("one thing")'. This means that everything is one; earth and all elements and even God. Walter A. Elwell, *Evangelical Dictionary of Theology* (Grand Rapids: Baker Books, 1984), p. 730.

[17] Elwell, *Evangelical Dictionary of Theology*, p. 861: 'Polytheism: The belief in a multitude of distinct and separate deities. It is formally contrasted with pantheism, the belief in an impersonal God identical with the universe, although the two doctrines can sometimes be found in the same religious tradition.'

[18] Pantheism: 'The word, coming from the Greek pan and theos, means "everything is God". It was coined by John Toland in 1705 to refer to philosophical systems that tend to identify God with the world' (Elwell, *Evangelical Dictionary of Theology*, p. 820). All the varieties of pantheism differ from the indigenous view of Creator because it denies 'the transcendence of God, advocating his radical immanence' (Elwell, *Evangelical Dictionary of Theology*, p. 821). While indigenous people recognize the spirit of God in creation, they also acknowledge the Creator, the One who made everything.

at the same time understanding that there is a huge difference between human life and animal life.

The indigenous, as believers in Creator, are between Deists[19] and
Theists. Deists perceive a God who is distant and yet deserves respect and reverence while Theism is simply, '... belief in the existence of God'.[20] Deists believe in a Supreme Being who created the
universe but is not connected nor interested in planet Earth. Deism
is the opposite of monism and pantheism.

Is God transcendent? Yes, He is beyond one's imagination. He
is His own person, separate from the world and in no way intricate-
ly tied to it (to humankind), expect by His own love.

Within indigenous thought, Creator is not a proper name but rather a descriptive name. Indigenous people do not presume to
name the One who made everything. All of the various designations
for Creator are descriptions – The Great Spirit (Cree), The Great
Mystery (Sioux), The One up on high (Carrier/Dakelh), Grandfather (many Nations use this title to describe the Creator as the old-
est, most respected Elder akin to 'Ancient One' in Dan. 7.13). Elders have a respected place in First Nations worldview.

> Grandfather, Great Spirit, you have been always, and before you
> nothing has been. There is not one to pray to but you. The star
> nations all over the heavens are yours, and yours are the grasses
> of the earth. You are older than all need, older than all pain and
> prayer. Grandfather, Great Spirit, fill us with the light. Give us
> the strength to understand and the eyes to see. Teach us to walk

---

[19] Elwell, *Evangelical Dictionary of Theology*, p. 304, explains:

The basic doctrines of deism are: (1) the belief in a supreme being; (2) the obligation to worship, (3) the obligation of ethical conduct; (4) the need for repentance from sins; and (5) divine rewards and punishments in this life and
the next. These five points were stated by Lord Herbert, often called the father of deism. Deism contradicts orthodox Christianity by denying any direct
intervention in the natural order by God. Although deists profess belief in
personal providence, they deny the Trinity, the incarnation, the divine authority of the Bible, the atonement, miracles, any particular elect people such as
Israel, and any supernatural redemptive act in history.

[20] Elwell, *Evangelical Dictionary of Theology*, p. 1080.

the soft earth as relatives to all that live. Help us, for without you we are nothing. (Sioux prayer)[21]

A Dakelh elder named Lizette Hall wrote a book called *The Carrier My people*.[22] In her book she explains beliefs taught to her by her father as passed down by her grandfather. Although the name *Yudughu* is not in the book, it means the *Being up on High*.[23] Lizette herself told the author the following a few years before her death:[24]

> When there was a storm, and the children mentioned it, they were told not to talk about it as they were not old enough, because it was the 'Up on high' who was doing it. They knew something watched over them. They respected the weather and their environment. When the sun came out after the rain, a person threw a piece of cold ember from the fireplace to another person across the fire to attract their attention, and point to the sun without saying a word.[25]

Perhaps there were no written laws or commandments etched in stone but there was a sense of what is right and good.

> They lived as sensibly as they could. Their lives were orderly, and methodical. They advised one another. If, anyone heard another one talk bad, or do something wrong, he was told it was not right, because 'the up on high' did not like it.[26]

Indigenous people learned all they knew from keen observation of the earth and the stories passed down from generation to generation. 'For since the creation of the world God's invisible qualities – his eternal power and divine nature – have been clearly seen, being understood from what has been made, so that men are without excuse' (Rom. 1.20).

---

[21] Lyn Klug, *Soul Weavings: A Gathering of Women's Prayers* (Minneapolis: Augsburg, 1996), p. 88.

[22] Carrier is the former name given to the Dakelh, but Dakelh is how they have always described themselves.

[23] Hall, *The Carrier My People*, p. 7.

[24] Lizette, a living history book, was introduced to the author by John and Shannpn Bell Wyminga, Presbyterian ministers among the Nazko nation (Dakelh).

[25] Hall, *The Carrier My People*, p. 7.

[26] Hall, *The Carrier My People*, p. 10.

Creator and Creation - Theology of the Land

This part of the theology section will address the indigenous view of Mother Earth and the sacredness of the Earth. It will provide a framework for understanding these views through the lens of Scripture and Christian thought. Quoting Chief Seattle, Suqwamish and Duwamish (1786-1866):

> We know that the white man does not understand our ways. One portion of the land is the same to him as the next, for he is a stranger who comes in the night and takes from the land whatever he needs. The earth is not his brother, but his enemy – and when he has conquered it, he moves on. He leaves his fathers' graves, and his children's birthright is forgotten.[27]

Most often misunderstood about indigenous people is spirituality. Although, the word 'spirituality' can be construed by almost anyone to mean almost anything, to indigenous people in Canada and the United States it generally denotes a belief in the Creator and recognition of the spirit world. While these beliefs can be different based on each family within each Nation, they commonly involve these two main themes.

Many teachers do not always know about indigenous spirituality because of their field of study, lack of interest, or lack of contact with an indigenous person. More colleges and universities are, however, inviting First Nations to share information on indigenous religion, worldview, and beliefs.

An example of unawareness, presented in the Background and Significance section of Chapter 1, is a bible college teacher who claimed a totem pole[28] was an idol. Totem poles are not idols but rather relate a story of a family, a clan, a great chief, or they may also serve as a signpost to lead one to a good fishing spot. The people erect them to remember and honor these stories. This lack of insight can extend over many areas of Native worldview but spirituality is the foremost. First Nations Christians always find them-

---

[27] Kent Nerburn, *The Wisdom of Native Americans* (Novato, CA: New World Library, 1999), p. 45. Quoting Chief Seattle (1786-1866) from the Suqwamish and Duwamish tribe.

[28] The totem pole was from the North West coast (North West coast denotes indigenous people from Alaska, British Columbia, and Washington).

selves defending their Native ancestral beliefs and grow weary of the constant questioning. Either indigenous Christians will accept the idea that their culture is substandard (to the dominant Christian culture) and both cultures reject it all, or they will learn ways that the beauty of Native culture can be communicated to the church and used for the glory of God. The Bible gives reference to the fact that other nations offer incense to the Lord, "'In every place incense and pure offerings will be brought to me, because my name will be great among the nations", says the Lord Almighty' (Mal. 1.11).

In the past, Christians tended to marginalize Native beliefs as wicked and the opposite of Christianity. However, the respect for indigenous knowledge is growing and even creation, which indigenous people view as sacred, is being discussed. There has always been a certain amount of respect given to indigenous people by environmental groups but sometimes they can be destructive by perpetuating myths about First Nations. Quoting David Waller regarding the marginalizing of Native people by environmentalism:

> A classic case was that weeping Indian television ad of two decades ago: A Native American man in traditional dress surveys environmental havoc. A tear runs down his cheek. The image should be ambiguous, but it is not. It should cause us to consider both the destruction of his environment and the destruction of his people, but it does not. We should think for a moment that he might be weeping in memory of all the cultural destruction that was predicated on land theft and environmental recklessness – the destruction of people and interpersonal relationships, the disease, the genocide, the boarding school terrorism, alcoholism, unemployment, the theft of language – but we do not. No, we see immediately that the Indian weeps because white people do not pick up after themselves. This advertisement represents the way in which environmentalism has marginalized the Indian.[29]

---

[29] From David Waller's contribution entitled: 'Friendly Fire: When Environmentalists Dehumanize American Indians', cited by Duane Champagne (Turtly Mountain Chippewa) (ed.), *Contemporary Native American Cultural Issues* (Walnut Creek, CA: AltaMira Press, 1999), p. 289.

This marginalization happens on theological levels as well. There are many false beliefs about indigenous spirituality. The ambiguous nature of indigenous spirituality causes many Christian missionaries to disapprove of any Native customs, regalia, songs, dances, ceremonies, and even the old stories. As Walking Buffalo, Stoney from Alberta, Canada (1871-1967) puts it:

> We saw the Great Spirit's work in almost everything: sun, moon, trees, wind, and mountains. Sometimes we approached Him through these things. Was that so bad? ... Did you know that trees talk? Well they do. They talk to each other, and they'll talk to you if you listen. Trouble is white people don't listen. They never learned to listen to the Indians so I don't suppose they'll listen to other voices in nature. But I have learned a lot from trees: sometimes about the weather, sometimes about animals, sometimes about the Great Spirit.[30]

In Isa. 55.12, the Bible also talks about the trees clapping their hands and the psalmist states, 'the heavens declare the glory of God' (Ps. 19.1). Nature can teach people what most overlook in their insulated and isolated modern world. However, the Stoney from Alberta also shows us that Creation reveals its Creator through, as described in theological terms, Natural Theology.[31]

The Earth is sacred. It is sacred because it is from the Creator's hand. The sacredness does not result from the beauty of creation alone but from the beauty of Creator's touch. No one can behold the intricacies found in nature and assume there is no God, unless they have not paid sufficient attention. Indigenous people have always been close to the land because the oral tradition of the people tells them that they were placed here by the Creator.

Indigenous people believe that the Creator gave the land to them to care for and enjoy, not to 'own', but to share. They do not believe that anyone owns the land in the English 'common-law' property ownership sense, but in the sense that Creator owns the land and it yields sustenance and subsistence for His creation: people, animals, trees, every living thing. Psalm 24.1 states, 'The earth is the Lord's, and everything in it, the world, and all who live in it'. All

---

[30] Cited in Fitzgerald, *Indian Spirit*, p. 7.

[31] Duffield and Van Cleave, *Foundations of Pentecostal Theology*, p. 49.

indigenous people believe that Creator placed them on their land for a purpose. That purpose ties indigenous people to the land. Creator gave indigenous people a mandate to care for the land. The Bible uses the word 'steward' the land which was a mandate given to Adam in Gen. 1.28 and as is stated in *The Message*, 'Prosper! Reproduce! Fill Earth! Take charge! Be responsible for fish in the sea and birds in the air, for every living thing that moves on the face of Earth.'[32] Eugene Peterson uses more appropriate verbiage than the NIV, when he says 'Take Charge' and 'Be responsible' which means *get busy taking care of the earth*, whereas in the NIV *subdue* conveys a connotation of dominion which is solely attributed to God. God never said, 'this land is yours'; he said, 'the world earth and every tree that has fruit with seed in it will be yours for food' (Gen. 1.29). Trees, plants, and fruit are for food, not to own. In verse 30, the Creator gives beasts, birds, and all creatures green plants for food. Nowhere does He say the earth is yours. No one can own the land anymore than anyone can own the air or the sun that shines, or the rains that falls. Tecumseh, Shawnee (1768-1813) stated: 'No tribe has the right to sell, even to each other, much less to strangers ... Sell a country! Why not sell the air, the great sea, as well as the earth? Didn't the Great Spirit make them all for the use of his children?'[33]

'The Lord God formed the man from the dust of the ground and breathed into his nostrils the breath of life, and the man became a living being' (Gen. 2.7). Indigenous people believe and understand that humans and animals are a special part of creation because they share breath. Some indigenous persons believe animals are not a crucial part of creation. However, when God flooded the earth, every species of animal was invited into the ark. God preserved them because He loves His creation and not simply for sustenance for Noah's family. Also notice when God blessed man in Gen. 1.28 with food he also gave the animals the same blessing. When God said to rule over the animals, He was giving them a royal decree not to rule with the idea of conquering, but as He rules, with justice, considering what is best for them. At this point God

---

[32] Eugene Peterson, *The Message: The Bible in Contemporary Language* (Colorado Springs: NavPress, 2002).

[33] Nerburn, *The Wisdom of Native Americans* p. 41. Quoting Tecumseh from the Shawnee tribe.

does not give humankind the right to eat animals because green food is bountiful.

Native people say that everything is related, 'all' meaning plant, animal, and elements. This statement does not infer pantheism[34] but is actually quite scientific. Scientists advocate that the systems of the Earth are all connected and people are utterly dependent on the Earth. The trees and plants take toxins and change them into oxygen while evaporation and condensation provide the Earth's water cycle. It is a fact that people are dependent upon these systems for their survival. Indigenous people say the same thing as the Scientists when they recognize that they are one with the Earth. Indians do not have an attitude of

> man over against space, or over against nature as two implacable foes, one of whom must be victorious, master over the other. He sees man in nature, part of nature, living with it rather than on top of it.[35]

Mother Earth is very important to Native people. They, like most Christian environmentalists, sense the Sacred in creation. Native people recognize the Spirit in the Earth, not the *spirit of the Earth*, but the Holy Spirit infused into creation. Mother Earth is not a god or a being but rather a creation of the Creator. People can become confused because the Spirit is so close to creation, as is the spirit world (close), therefore some can mistakenly believe that the Earth has power of its own, whereas the power is actually the Holy Spirit infused in Creation.

Regarding the divinization of the Earth, N.T. Wright gives insight to the Apostle Paul's view,

> This is one of the most basic things that a pagan audience would have picked up: Paul stood over against the multiplicity of gods with the news of the one God, and stood over against the divinization of creation with the news of the createdness of creation

---

[34] '... from the Greek *pan* and *theos*, means "everything is God"' (Elwell, *Evangelical Dictionary of Theology*, p. 820).

[35] Hugo Muller, *Why Don't You? A Look At Attitudes Towards Indians* (Toronto: Anglican Publications, 1972), p. 13.

– without any suggestion that creation was therefore less than good.[36]

The Earth is good and tells the story of Creator. Clues to the artist are found in the artwork. The Bible teaches that God created man from the dust of the earth. Humorously, a scientist tells God, 'We've learned how to create life and I challenge you to a duel. Whoever creates life first wins'. The scientist then kneels down to scoop some dust and God says, 'Wait a minute, get your own dust'.

Every Christian knows the Biblical story of how God created humanity. Everyone also knows that when people die, bodies naturally turn to dust. The Earth[37] is part of one's human fabric and therefore one metaphorically refers to it as his or her Mother.

However, the term Mother Earth can cause some anxiety for those who do not understand the meaning. Mother Earth maintains life through its attributes, water being the most important. Like a good mom, Mother Earth provides water, food, (moisture, and oxygen), and the land provides shelter but Mother Earth is sustained by Creator. There is a difference between matter (all of creation) and the Creator. Every indigenous person will acknowledge this and open indigenous gatherings[38] with prayer. Native people recognize the Spirit in the Earth, not the spirit of the Earth, but the Holy Spirit infused into creation.

Indigenous people recognize the sacred in the Earth and some believe it has a spirit or spirits. However, the Creator animates creation and any sense of the sacred in creation is simply the Creator.

Placement Theology
First Nations identify each other by place. This is the opposite of customary identification in North America. When North Americans meet they will typically ask, 'What do you do?' This question gives much information to the person inquiring, e.g. rank, social, and

---

[36] N.T. Wright, *What Saint Paul Really Said* (Grand Rapids: Eerdmans, 1997), p. 87.

[37] Earth is capitalized because it is being used as a proper name like Saturn or Mars and out of respect because the Earth is the Lord's (Ps. 24.1) and humanity is its steward.

[38] Gatherings such as Powwow's, feasts, Potlatches, funerals, memorials, and sweats.

economic status. For example if someone is a doctor they are worthy of more respect than someone less educated or less honorable.

Native people initiate conversations with this question, 'Where are you from?' The question does not mean what town you currently live in and Native people automatically know the correct answer is to name a Nation and Reservation, e.g. 'I am Chiricahua Apache from San Carlos Reservation'. Their identity comes from their land and the land connects them to their relatives. Without land, they are not a people.

Divine Placement

Divine Placement Theology may be defined as the reconciliation between the Biblical record and traditional First Nations records of the Creator's original placement of the people on the land and His intended purposes for them.

Every First Nation has within its recorded history the concept of the 'People of the Land'. Even the name by which most Nations identify themselves is usually translated as a variation of 'The People' or 'The People of the Land'.

Every First Nation believes that Creator placed them exactly where they are. This belief is true of all First Nations people and is exemplified by The Assembly of First Nations, which is a gathering of Grand Chiefs from all across Canada. The first item on The Charter[39] of the Assembly of First Nations states, 'We the Chiefs of the Indian First Nations in Canada having declared: that *our peoples are the original peoples of this land having been put here by the Creator*'.[40] It was a sovereign placement by God. All the creation stories record the truth of Divine Placement.

The Chief of Saik'uz First Nation, Stanley Thomas[41] told the Dakelh story of creation. He said Creator placed people here and gave them this land to take care of. He placed it in their custody. The host people of the Carrier lands must be responsible for its care. The Chief was upset because some people took the land and did terrible things such as build dams and change the direction of

---

[39] This is a consolidation of the original AFN Charter adopted in 1985 and subsequent amendments up to 2003.

[40] Taken from the website of the Assembly of First Nations: http://www.afn.ca/article.asp?id=57 (emphasis added).

[41] In the year 2000.

rivers. His own Reserve, Saik'uz, once had a strong river flowing through it but now there is only a small creek because of the Kenny Dam.[42] Chief Stanley said one day Creator will return and make things right. Creator will look at what people have done to the earth and will make things right.

In Genesis 6 through 9 one reads the story about Noah who along with his wife, three sons, and three daughters-in-law survived a catastrophic world-wide flood. Many of the First Nations stories tell of this event, usually with a slight variation due to different cultural perceptions. For example, the people of the Northwest coast of British Columbia tell of how eight people survived the flood in a great canoe. Their conceptualization of the story did not allow for an 'ark', but a canoe was an understandable concept to them.

They accurately retold the correct number of the people in the canoe/ark and other significant details. This is consistent with oral tradition. Oral tradition typically does not always recount the exact story every time but there are always consistencies throughout as is exemplified in the various parables related by the three authors of the synoptic Gospels. They add or ignore various details of a story but there are words that agree verbatim. Some of the parables have double agreement and some have triple agreement meaning that all three synoptic Gospels have the same wording.[43]

Oral tradition is the reason we have the Torah. Moses recorded the stories of Israel through the use of oral tradition. The reason that the content of the Bible exists is because someone wrote it down – especially the gospels, which tell the story of Jesus.

In Gen. 11.1-9 one reads of Noah's descendents who rapidly multiplied but did not obey God's directives to fill the earth, preferring rather to stay and build a tower to heaven, thus disobeying the express will of God. This disobedience caused God to exercise His sovereignty and supernaturally transfer them in various numbers to the remotest parts of the globe (Gen. 11.8, 9). The Hebrew word *putz*, which is translated 'scattered' in English translations has in its meaning the ideas of 'casting abroad' or 'dispersing'. Therefore Gen. 11.9b can be translated as, 'From (Babel) the Lord dispersed

---

[42] The Kenny Dam also flooded the ancient Carrier village called Cheslatta where Alec George was originally from (the author's grandfather).

[43] Kurt Aland, *Synopsis Quattor Evangeliorum* (Stuttgart: Deutsche Bibelgesellschaft, 15th edn, 1996).

them over the face of the whole earth'. This conveys the idea that God supernaturally placed the people where He wanted them to be which correlates with the Apostle Paul's words in Acts 17.26, 'From one man he made every nation of men, that they should inhabit the whole earth; and He determined the times set for them and the exact places where they should live'.

This truth is one of the commonly held beliefs of every First Nation. How is it that all First Nations have stories about the Creator placing them exactly where they now live and are adamant that they did not travel from Asia on a long-ago-sunken land bridge through Mongolia and Alaska? They did not get to their land by walking all the way from the Middle East, through Asia, and into Canada and then south to Argentina. The Creator placed them exactly where they live because He purposed and predestined places for them to live.

This leads to a discussion of the Divine purpose in the Divine placement of First Nations. Acts 17.27, 28 shed some light on the purposes that Creator had in mind. 'God did this so men would seek Him and perhaps reach out for Him and find Him, though He is not far from each one of us. For in Him we live and move and have our being.'

It was the Creator's intention for First Nations people to understand Him through His attributes as revealed to them in the land. They then would reach out and love Him in return. Creator was all around them, in their living, moving, and being. What was their 'living, moving, and being'? It was their *environment* and their *culture*.

Worshipping Creator in the Environment
The beauty and diversity of the Land displayed the beauty and diversity of Creator. Respecting the Land was equivalent to respecting the Creator. Seeing Creator in the creation was Divine revelation. As Ohiyesa, Charles Eastman, in Wahpeton Dakota (1858-1939) put it:

> Whenever, in the course of the daily hunt, the red hunter comes upon a scene that is strikingly beautiful and sublime – a black thunder-cloud with the rainbow's glowing arch above the mountain; a white waterfall in the heart of a green gorge; a vast prairie tinged with the blood-red of sunset – he pauses for an instant in

the attitude of worship. He sees no need for setting apart one day in seven as a holy day, since to him all days are God's.[44]

The land, bountiful in food, was a revelation of Creator's providence. The mountains, rivers, forests, and the plains spoke of His Majesty. The animals reflected the strong, and yet gentle attributes of a powerful, protecting, and loving God.

Worshipping Creator in the Culture

Language

The diversity of language reflected the diversity of the Land. Creator god gave both as gifts. Communication was essential to fellowship. Fellowship and love among brothers was an essential prerequisite to love of God. Language when understood, communicates the feeling of the soul and the stories of Divine truth and revelation.

Instruments

Instruments indigenous to the land were used to accompany songs. A rich diversity of instruments was created from objects of the Land. Percussion was taken from animal skin drums, logs, dirt, and clay; flues from wood and reed; string vibrato from sinew. Songs were reflections of the depths of human experience in joy, mourning, love, anger, and worship.

Native songs have always been sung in a minor key. While major keys are very sharp and clear, minor keys tend to be mysterious and indistinct. Music teachers instruct that nature sings in the minor key.

Regalia

Clothing was originally given to the first man and woman as a covering for their nakedness. God make them clothing from animal skin. The resultant shed blood became a spiritual covering for their sin. Clothing is a type of atonement. Richness of story and meaning can be communicated through the beautiful regalia of First Nations. The elders of the Northwest Coast First Nations speak of the significance of the colors in the wearing of beautiful button blankets.

---

[44] Fitzgerald, *Indian Spirit*, p. 87.

The color red was derived from a mixture utilizing actual animal blood.

Art Forms

Various First Nations art forms celebrate the richness of life from Creator. The art gives life to Native stories and honor to families and relatives who have passed away. The art forms are a way of keeping stories alive and remembering traditions.

Social Customs

Social customs are the central part of the community. There are societal rules from stories that are understood and upheld as strict moral codes. The Creator is the basis for most of these customs because of the high respect Native people have for Creator. Other gatherings are memorials, weddings, and each clan has responsibilities.

The Darkening of Romans 1.21

The book of Romans tells of a darkening that took place in every culture of the world, including First Nations. In Rom. 1.23 true worship of the Creator was exchanged for idolatry. Marriage, which reflected God's relationship with humankind, was exchanged for lust and immorality (v. 24), and Divine Revelation was abandoned for false teaching and lies (v. 25). Every people and nation fell into these sins.

The Remnant

In spite of the deviation of *the darkening* of a people and cultures, there were always signs that the people once knew the truth, '... they knew God' (Rom. 1.21). Deep in the heart of every person, in the basis of every culture, and in the foundation of their stories, beliefs, and traditions there is the belief in the One, True God – The Creator. Every First Nations has a descriptive name for Creator. These names elicit respect and awe from even the most darkened heart.

Abraham was an example of a man who looked beyond the darkening of his culture and was an obedient servant and friend of God (Gen. 12.1). These people are the *Remnant.* They have always lived among our people, telling the stories of the Creator, prophetically looking forward to a day when a fuller revelation of the Creator would come. Some stories told of a 'book' of truth, still other stories told of the Creator's Son. When it came to indigenous people, these remnants of true worshippers were among the first to embrace the fuller revelation of God from the pages of the Bible.

First Nations are called to be guardians of the Land so that it might forever continue to declare the glory of God. This responsibility as stewards and hosts of this land has never been given away. It is the unique commission from Creator. The Land may be shared, but First Nations role as the Hosts and protectors of the Land is Divinely instituted and cannot be changed.

First Nations must be careful to preserve, maintain, and practice their unique cultures. Language, music, art forms, dance, and regalia are to continue to reflect God's original purposes for them.

Holy Spirit

The Spirit was present during creation as Ps. 104.30 states, 'When you send your Spirit, they are created, and you renew the face of the earth'. There are many scriptural symbols of the Holy Spirit such as oil,[45] water (Exod. 17.6; Ezek. 36.25-27; 47.1; Jn 3.5; 4.14; 7.38, 39), dove (Lk. 3.22), wind (Ezek. 27.7-10; Jn 3.8; Acts 2.2),[46] cloud (Exod. 13.21),[47] and fire (Isa. 4.4; Mt. 3.11; Lk. 3.16).[48]

God also spoke to Moses through a burning bush. When the bush spoke to Moses he did not try to analyze the source, he simply answered and heard the voice of Creator through the flaming, talking tree. These are the stories to which indigenous people can relate and enjoy.

It is normative for Christians to accept the symbolism of the Holy Spirit in the form of a dove. However, it is more difficult to accept the idea of a Spirit-infused creation where Creator speaks

---

[45] 'Oil is perhaps the most familiar and common symbol of the Spirit. Whenever oil was used ritually in the Old Testament it spoke of usefulness, fruitfulness, beauty, life, and transformation.' Myer Pearlman, *Knowing the Doctrines of the Bible* (Springfield, MO: Gospel Publishing House, 1937), p. 290.

[46] 'Wind symbolizes the regenerative work of the Spirit and is indicative of His mysterious, independent, penetrating, life-giving and purifying operation.' Pearlman, *Knowing the Doctrines of the Bible*, p. 289.

[47] 'By day the Lord went ahead of them in a pillar of cloud to guide them on their way and by night in a pillar of fire to give them light, so that they could travel by day or night.'

[48] Pearlman, *Knowing the Doctrines of the Bible*, p. 288.

through animals, water, and trees (Job 12.7-9). The Bible talks about the trees clapping their hands (Isa. 55.12) and the heavens declaring the glory of God (Ps. 19.1). Nature can teach many things that most people overlook in their insulated and isolated modern world. The Holy Spirit can choose to speak through whatever means, wherever, and whenever He desires. Creation reveals its Creator to man through, as is said in theological terms, Natural Theology.[49]

The Holy Spirit allowed a donkey to speak to Balaam in Numbers 22. The Scriptures point out that God opened the donkey's mouth. Here is yet another example where an Israelite does not flinch or react to a talking entity (especially one that does not normally talk). Instead of being afraid and running away or asking someone, 'Can you hear this?' Balaam has an entire conversation, even an intimate one, with his donkey. The donkey asks Balaam two questions, both of which Balaam answers un-hesitantly. The second question in Num. 22.30 is the intimate one, '... Am I not your own donkey, which you have always ridden, to this day? Have I been in the habit of doing this to you?' Prior to this the donkey had stopped and Balaam beat the donkey three times. Then Balaam answers, 'No' and finally recognizes the reason the donkey had stopped; there was an angel on the roadway the donkey had seen but Balaam had not noticed. Animals seem to have an ability to perceive things that humans cannot see. The angel then scolds Balaam for not listening to his donkey and states that the animal saved Balaam's life.

The Holy Spirit is another comforter,[50] just as Jesus was a comforter, but the Spirit's actions, are different from those of Jesus. The Holy Spirit is a teacher and guide, and allows one to discern their sin and need for cleansing. The word used by many traditional indigenous people when they pray is, 'Creator have pity on us'. Pity is the word used for mercy because they recognize the need for cleansing. The Holy Spirit reveals to sinners the need for cleansing.

Anyone who has spent time in jail knows the definition of the word convict. It is a legal term with dual meanings; a person who has committed a crime and the act of declaring someone guilty of a

---

[49]Duffield and Van Cleave, *Foundation of Pentecostal Theology*, p. 49.

[50]Duffield and Van Cleave, *Foundation of Pentecostal Theology*, p. 285.

crime in a court of law.[51] Jesus used this terminology when He described the coming of the promised Holy Spirit,

> But I tell you the truth: It is for your good that I am going away. Unless I go away, the Counselor[52] will not come to you; but if I go, I will send him to you. When he comes, he will convict the world of guilt[53] in regard to sin and righteousness and judgment: in regard to sin, because men do not believe in me (Jn 16.7-9).

Jesus used legal jargon because that was the nature of the Jewish relationship with God, established through the laws given to Moses. This reflects the culture in the time of Jesus. Can one take the law language from Jesus' culture and adapt it to a culture that does not embrace moral laws based on Judeo-Christian tenets? Here is where missiology must step in as the wise older brother and suggest that, 'yes, it can be done'.

The beautiful characteristic is that the Holy Spirit is a teacher. '… He will guide you into all truth …' (Jn 16.13). This cannot be accomplished absent community. Without community, there are no boundaries for the person trying to figure it all out. Once again, it is imperative that the theological community work together with First Nations towards self-theologizing in order for the gospel to be disseminated in the most productive and constructive manner.

Water, Fire, Smoke – Indigenous Perspective on the Holy Spirit

Christianity teaches that Creator infuses creation, however, there is a point where Creator stops and creation begins. It appears to indigenous people that elements, wood, stone, plants, and animals have mystical qualities. What is the explanation? Creator certainly does infuse creation and what indigenous people perceive is not the spirit within the object itself, but rather the Spirit of God in another dimension, or as they say 'the spirit world', that saturates this present reality. Although there are some Native people who may believe that objects have a spirit, more often than not indigenous people in the United States and Canada believe that Creator is *other*

---

[51] Microsoft Word Dictionary, 2007.

[52] Taken from the Greek word παρακλητος (*parakletos*) meaning Advocate. Duffield and Van Cleave, *Foundation of Pentecostal Theology*, p. 285.

[53] Or will expose the guilt of the world (Duffield and Van Cleave, *Foundation of Pentecostal Theology*, p. 284).

than creation while deeply caring for it. The words *other than* are used instead of *above* because it infers that God and therefore humans are far above creation thus diminishing man's responsibility to care for it.

This quote from Myer Pearlman encapsulates indigenous thought,

> The Holy Spirit is revealed in the Old Testament in three ways: first, as the creative or cosmic Spirit through whose power the universe and all living creatures were created; second, as the dynamic or power-giving Spirit; third, as the regenerative Spirit by which human nature is changed.[54]

One can glean from this simple overview of the doctrine of the Holy Spirit that there are ways to bridge the gap of misunderstanding between indigenous people and theologians. This project is not an exhaustive study on indigenous theology but rather presents comparative points where indigenous faith can intersect with Christianity. This project is an introduction to indigenous worldview, concepts, and ministry.

The Great Mystery of the Incarnation

This title was used by a professor at Regent College who was referencing the Incarnation of Christ during preaching class.[55] Darrell Johnson may not have been aware that one of the descriptive indigenous names of Creator is the Great Mystery but it made a great impression on this author and also gave significant weight to the subject matter.

The word Incarnation literally means *in the flesh,*[56] that Jesus is fully human and fully God.

> In the context of Christian theology, the act whereby the eternal Son of God, the Second Person of the Holy Trinity, without ceasing to be what he is, God the Son, took into union with

---

[54] Pearlman, *Knowing the Doctrines of the Bible*, pp. 290-91.

[55] Regent College, Vancouver, BC, Canada: 'Preaching' by Darrell Johnson, Fall 2002.

[56] Elwell, *Evangelical Dictionary of Theology*, p. 555.

himself what he before that act did not possess, a human nature.[57]

The Incarnation to Native people means that Jesus has come into their world and revealed Creator, not that Creator revealed Jesus. Jesus the Messiah points to Creator.

Jesus reveals the Creator, the Great Spirit, the Great Mystery. Indigenous people need to see Jesus clearly. Or does Creator reveal Himself? The Creator, The Great Spirit is seen in the face of Jesus Christ. Does Creator show Himself? There Creator is a universal spirit and is the Great Spirit. Creator is a Spirit. Indigenous people recognize this Great Creator as a spirit. A spirit is invisible and not apprehend-able. No one can see the Spirit, nor touch the Spirit. When First Nations called the Creator – The Great Spirit or The Great Mystery – their theology was correct.

However, humans are flesh, and bone, and blood. How then can this Creator, Great Spirit reveal Himself to those who are limited by sight, hearing, touch, smell and taste? One cannot utilize one's senses to comprehend the Being up on High.

One realizes something of the Creator through nature. Similarly to the ancient Hebrew understanding, native people have always felt the presence of the Creator in the wind, smoke, water, and fire. This symbolism is found throughout the Torah.[58] 'I have often felt the presence of the Great Spirit on the Nadleh River that runs through my reserve. I have heard the call of the Great Mystery as the wind pushes through the trees.'[59]

However, nature cannot fully reveal the Great Spirit. Nature can give us great lessons and tell of the majesty and greatness of our Creator and even how Creator works, but nature cannot tell us if Creator loves us. Is this Creator a God of love?

Secondly, Creator has spoken through our Elders, teachers, and prophets. The Dakelh[60] Elders have told the author that Creator 'has placed us on our land'. The Carrier Nation is given great re-

---

[57] Elwell, *Evangelical Dictionary of Theology*, p. 555.

[58] Commonly known as the Old Testament. The word 'Torah' is used here to honor the Jewish tradition.

[59] From a poem called 'Presence', by Cheryl Bear-Barnetson, 2008.

[60] Also known as the Carrier Nation from northern British Columbia, Canada.

sponsibility to steward the land of their ancestors. These stories are passed down from generation to generation. Prophecy from Creator is not exclusive to the Hebrew prophets in the Torah. Even the Bible testifies that other prophets can seek truth. Even the Magi came from the East (Mt. 2.1).

Teachers, Elders, and prophets can all speak about the Great Spirit but they are human themselves, subject to all the same limitations which sometimes results in the message being distorted.

> Randy Woodley's (Keetoowah Cherokee) version of Hebrews 1:1-3, 'Long ago, Creator spoke many times and in many ways to our ancestors through the prophets. But now in these final days, he has spoken to us through his Son. Creator promised everything to the Son as an inheritance, and through the Son he made the universe and everything in it. The Son reflects Creator's own glory, and everything about him represents Creator exactly. He sustains the universe by the mighty power of his command.'[61]

Thirdly, Christians believe God spoke to humanity through a book. But 'revelation cannot come perfectly through a book' as E. Stanley Jones says because, 'literature cannot rise higher than life'.[62] Literature is not life, one needs THE LIFE.

So then, the only method of receiving complete revelation, especially for First Nations, is through a life, a character, a person that depicts for humanity the essence of God. The full and complete revelation of God was given to people – not just in nature, or in sayings and stories, nor perfectly in the Bible, although the Bible is God's word, the Bible is not *the* revelation of God, it is the inspired record of the revelation.

Creator's perfect revealing to the Native people is in Jesus Christ, the man who was also Creator, the God-man, or the Great Spirit man. Jesus fully shows the heart, mind, character, will, and life of the Creator.

John 1.14 states, 'The Word became flesh and dwelt among us'. The Word here is used to describe Jesus. The word *dwelt* translates

---

[61] Randy Woodley (Keetoowah Cherokee), *When Going to Church is Sin: And Other Essays on Native American Christian Missions* (Scotland, PA: Healing the Land Publishers, 2007), p. 27.

[62] E. Stanley Jones, *Abundant Living* (New York: Abingdon-Cokesbury, 1942), p. 19).

directly as *tabernacled*. To say 'Jesus *tabernacled* among us' in the English language is awkward. However, that particular word emphasized something to the Hebrew people. The Tabernacle conjures up many wonderful recollections, even to the contemporary Hebrew mind. It reminds them of when Yahweh came and lived among their people. Yahweh had instructed them carefully as how to build a tabernacle and it served as a sign to their nation that God was with them. To say the Word became flesh and tabernacled among them meant that Yahweh had confined Himself to a human body instead a tabernacle and made his home among the people. Eugene Peterson in *The Message* brings great clarity, 'The Word became flesh and blood and moved into the neighborhood. We saw the glory with our own eyes, the one-of-a-kind glory, like Father, like Son' (Jn 1.14, 15).[63] Now indigenous people can say, 'The Word became flesh and blood and moved onto the Reservation'.[64]

Later in Jn 14.8, the disciples say to Jesus, 'Show us the Father and that will be enough for us'. In other words, 'we will be satisfied'. If one could somehow see this Great Spirit, one's hearts would be satisfied. If Native people could see this Great Spirit it would fulfill a great longing. They want to know their Creator, The Great Spirit, this Great Mystery. The reason indigenous people have many cleansing ceremonies is to make a path to walk with the Creator. By performing these ceremonies, indigenous people acknowledge the impasse between Creator and themselves. They easily acknowledge that there is a great gulf between them and Creator because of the respect shown in not assigning a proper name to Creator.

In Jn 14.9, Jesus answered the question posed by his disciples by stating, 'anyone who sees me has seen the Creator'. Jesus answers the disciples longing, man's longing, and indigenous peoples' longing to know Creator.

The greatest thing one can say to indigenous people is that to know Jesus is to know the Creator, to love Jesus is to love the Creator, and to serve Jesus is to serve Creator. Creator was imperfectly revealed until now being perfectly revealed in Christ.

---

[63] Peterson, *The Message*, p. 185.
[64] The author's contextualized paraphrase of Jn 1.14.

Because the Creator, the Great Spirit is Jesus, humanity now understands more about the Creator. First Nations people can discern more about Creator. They recognize that Creator is good; that He loves people like Jesus loves people. They know that Creator gave himself for humanity because Jesus gave Himself, even sacrificing His life on the cross so that one day they might live and be resurrected with Him.

The Incarnation informs them that the Creator came into their world. That Jesus has come into the Indian world.

John 1.14, 'The word became flesh and blood and moved onto the reservation'. Jesus, the Great Mystery revealed, has moved onto the reservation and he must come to the indigenous person as an indigenous person. Not only has Jesus come into *the* world, he has come into the Native world. Sister Marie Archambault, one of the authors of the book *Native and Christian*, wrote about the first time she saw a First Nations minister who had long hair pulled back in a pony tail – she said she felt evangelized.

> The Lord Jesus Christ asserted the simplest and most profound statement regarding the mission of the Church: 'As the Father has sent me, I am sending you' (John 20:21, 17:18). Here Jesus defines the incarnational role of the disciples' mission; they are to be in the world in all the ways that He was present: aesthetically, culturally, politically, psychologically, and spiritually. As Jesus went into the world empowered by the perichoretic relationship within the Trinity, the *laos* of God are sent out with the resources of the Trinity and empowered by the perichoretic life of God.[65]

Jesus walks onto the reservation through this body, the church. The Incarnation means that the church must be an indigenous Church. It means that the message that is Christian must be an indigenous message. It also means that one's worship must be indigenous worship.

The church is the Incarnation of the Great Spirit on the reservations. Jesus fully came as a human being. The church must be fully indigenous to First Nations people. The church must be completely

---

[65] Cited by Mohanan Unni, 'Marketplace Ministry: Context for the Praxis of Spiritual Growth and Affirmation for the *Laos* of God' (DMin project, The King's Seminary, 2006), p. 107.

indigenous and authentic; worship, instruments, methods, institutions, and life. Now the church must take Jesus fully and authentically into the Native world.

The example Christ gives to those who are called to be missionaries in other cultures is that of humility. When Jesus came to this earth, he came as a human baby, which is the picture of utter vulnerability, completely dependent on others, growing and learning through the various stages of life.

> Your attitude should be the same as that of Christ Jesus: Who, being in very nature God, did not consider equality with God something to be grasped, but made himself nothing, taking the very nature of a servant, being made in human likeness. And being found in appearance as a man, he humbled himself and became obedient to death – even death on a cross (Phil. 2.5-8).

That is the heart of true Christianity and it means giving one's very life for those one serves just as Christ gave His. This leads one to the missiology section where one will discuss Paul's missionary endeavor to the Gentiles in the book of Acts. The missiology section gives further proof that one needs to walk humbly, not being ethnocentric or using cultural superiority, as one ministers to other cultures.

Missiological Considerations

Indigenous people in Canada and the United States have never heard the gospel of Jesus Christ. That is, the true gospel, because the gospel they first heard came with conquest, land acquisition, and was always equated with civilization. This is not the way it was supposed to be. However, the modern missions movement did not start till well after Columbus dug his heels into indigenous soil.

> … a thorough understanding of the meaning of culture is prerequisite to any effective communication of God's good news to a different people group.[66]

When the Europeans met indigenous people, the Europeans immediately felt superior.[67] They concluded that the Native Nations

---

[66] Winter and Hawthorne, *Perspectives on the World Christian Movement*, p. C-3.

were uncivilized when, in fact, they were very civilized and had many societal, cultural, and ceremonial precepts. Today the preaching of the gospel to Native people is based on other reasons, usually pity, but there are still underpinnings of assimilation.

> Contemporary Christians have a right to be concerned. In an increasingly secular, individualistic, and relativistic world – dubbed 'post-Christian' in the 1960's and now called 'post-modern' – the church is regularly viewed as irrelevant at best and Neanderthal at worst. Frankly, much of the blame lies with the church, especially those of us in the church who pride ourselves in being orthodox with regard to the historic faith. For all too often our orthodoxy has been either diluted by an unholy alliance with a given political agenda or diminished by legalistic or relativistic ethics quite unrelated to the character of God, or rendered ineffective by a pervasive rationalism in an increasingly un-rationalistic world.[68]

Central to the church's unholy alliance was a political agenda of assimilation and extermination of indigenous people. This is why Native people continue to reject the gospel of Jesus Christ. The church is irrelevant to many Native people because Christianity does not, in their mind, and usually in reality, fit into their Native worldview. True missions activity did not occur in Canada and the United States because of the political agenda working against Native people.

Today there are certain Korean churches and Jewish Messianic leaders who believe that indigenous people are originally from Korea or Israel. Perhaps they do not have a diabolical political agenda but they would rather believe Indians are Korean or Israeli than being interested in accepting Native people, their culture, and customs.

Koreans talk about the Bering Strait (Mongols/DNA etc.) and Hebrews discuss the Ten Lost Tribes of Israel (Diaspora), making comparisons, and showing similarities between the two cultures. Generally, when Korean people engage in outreach to Native peo-

---

[67] Devon A. Mihesuah, (Choctaw), *American Indians: Stereotypes and Realities* (Atlanta: Clarity Press, 2004), pp. 37-45.

[68] Gordon Fee, *Listening to the Spirit in the Text* (Grand Rapids: Eerdmans, 2000), p. xiii.

ple they say things like, 'We are so similar', or 'They are just like us'. Messianic Jewish leaders' gift Native people with shofars and prayer shawls, giving them items from a new culture and Koreans do not fully embrace Native culture because they believe theirs is superior. Both Korean and Hebrew cultures are beautiful but what is really going on here? It is actually simply another attempted assimilation. Just let indigenous people be.

Proper Missiology
When a church feels called to take a missionary team overseas, they will usually conduct some research before ever setting foot on foreign soil. Their pastor or leader will educate the team on rules or customs, give them some what-not-to-do's and perhaps an introduction to the language of the people they are visiting.

In Canada and the United States the soil is not what is foreign. For centuries the most important step in evangelism and missions has been overlooked. One could easily say that this does not matter – the Native people can speak English and they are Canadian/American so one can lay aside proper missiology. Non-Native people sometimes believe indigenous people to be American or Canadian simply because they live in America or Canada. This generalization is very damaging because Native people are from vastly different cultures. One needs to think missiologically about indigenous people of North America. Because indigenous people are often 'in our backyard' one can also assume that they are part of American/Canadian culture – or they should be. This is not an assimilation attempt but rather assimilation *assumed*.

If a non-Native pastor and their church truly desire to have any real spiritual effect on First Nations people, they must develop a new strategy because assimilation has not worked for the past 500 years. Instead, it has only made Native people angry and resentful toward the Church.

Contextualization
Is there such a thing as culturally appropriate evangelism? Evangelism strategies that claim to transcend all cultures because they are universal have been noted, however, this usually means that they have completely overlooked culture. Any missiologist who works in the realm of cultural sensitivity understands and teaches that the gospel is relevant to every culture.

Every pastor and leader knows there are such beasts as *inappro-priate* methods of evangelism and one cringes when thinking about the damage they do to the work of God. Inappropriate methods of evangelism have been evidenced in ministry to First Nations people for over 500 years starting with colonization and the Residential School, and ending with completely colonized Native churches.

What is contextualization of the gospel? It simply means putting the gospel in the context of the people to whom one is ministering. This is not an easy one-step process; it involves a substantial amount of work. Because each Nation has a unique culture, cus-toms, and language, the minister has his or her work cut out. For example, one should not take a big drum to a gathering of the Ca-hilla people because they use rattles handmade from gourds. They may have hand drums or allow their use but perhaps they feel more comfortable adhering to their own ways. Many tribes have translat-ed hymns in their languages. This is a beautiful expression of wor-ship but it is not contextualization, it is simply translation. Contex-tualization happens when the people themselves begin to write songs in their own style, with their unique instruments, and employ their language as worship to God. That is true contextualization.

The Huron Carol, a Christmas song written by Father Jean de Brébeuf in 1643, is a good example of contextualizing the gospel for indigenous people in Canada. He wrote this song for the Huron First Nation in a minor key using language and symbols commonly known.

> Contextualization is the process in which Christianity speaks to a group of people in language and symbols with which they are at home, and they in turn express their Christian faith within their culture. The model for this process is seen to be the Word of God, who became fully human in Jesus of Nazareth, who was incarnated in human flesh and in a particular history and cul-ture.[69]

Contextualization is the attempt of missionaries to be culturally sensitive to a people group. Although in Canadian (and American) history there were many mistakes made during the early missionary

[69] Bradley P. Holt, *Thirsty for God: A Brief History of Christian Spirituality* (Min-neapolis, MN: Fortress Press, 2005) p. 17.

endeavors, the Huron Carol represents a thread of the Incarnation. This Jesuit priest cared enough about the Huron people to make the gospel relevant to them.

In Acts, Hebrew Christianity is contextualized to fit Greek Gentiles (Acts 14). The issue of circumcision is a huge problem (at the Jerusalem Council) and Paul confronts the 'Judaizers' (Acts 15). Paul accuses them of adding to the gospel, of promoting their Hebrew culture over gospel freedom. He tells the council that Greeks do not need to become Jewish in order to be Christians – they can remain uncircumcised. Paul tells us that culture should not be an obstacle for one to come to Christ. Paul is yet again a shining example of contextualization when he explains God to the Greeks using their own unknown God (Acts 17.22-34).

Every letter Paul wrote was devoted to a specific people in a specific place at a specific time. He tailored each letter to the recipient thereby bringing about great illumination of the gospel. This is also a believer's responsibility – to bring the gospel to a specific people in a specific place at a specific time. One's worship needs to be in the language of the people. The missiological concept of contextualization is important in the First Nations church.

For First Nations in Canada and the United States, the gospel came hand in hand with fur traders, priests, marauding invaders, soldiers, residential schools, and the government. There are a few exceptions but generally Native people were treated like children.

In Canada, a segment of government is called the D.I.A.: the Department of Indians Affairs. This group is historically composed of non-native immigrants who make decisions on behalf of Indians, deciding what is best for them.

This group still exists today although First Nations have been fighting for autonomy over their own affairs. However, the government and the general public do not always trust First Nations as being competent to oversee their own affairs. There exists a condescending and patronizing attitude toward Native issues. Sadly, this is also often the attitude among church denominational leaders and pastors. Some denominations have their very own D.I.A. that makes decisions on behalf of Indians. They may feel they are doing their best for Native people but often are perceived as patronizing and arrogant. How can anyone assume they know what is best for another culture?

There are certain denominations that have taken a giant step *backwards* by placing First Nations ministry under the 'Multi-cultural' umbrella. The indigenous people of the land were here first and therefore everyone else belongs in the 'Multi-cultural' category. First Nations should not be placed under ethnic groups but should be shown honor. Their stories relate that the Creator placed them on their land. It is honorable to give First Nations a unique place because they were chosen by Creator to first be on this land.

Some of these denominations believe Native people are comparable to second generation immigrants. Many second generation immigrants often do not relate to the culture of their parents and desire to 'fit in' and adopt Canadian or American cultural identity. This often causes tension between parents and children. There are third generation immigrants, who, although they are 100 percent blood quantum of a certain ethnicity, have no connection whatsoever to their people or homeland. It is like a far away dream. They do not feel the connection nor do they miss this connection. This is the great tragedy of the New World. An indigenous person might ask them, 'Where are you from?' From an indigenous perspective this question is honoring to their place and their people. However, there are immigrants who are offended and say, 'I was born here and so were my parents! I'm American/Canadian!' Most indigenous people will wonder how someone can forget their homeland, the graves of their grandfathers, and the place of their people's origin.

First Nations, however, experience an identity struggle different from that of second or third-generation immigrants. Having been told for centuries that their culture, spirituality, and even language is from the devil – they struggle with being Indian in a Western society but are very proud to be indigenous people. In fact, the most important thing about them is their homeland.

Most First Nations equate colonization with Christianity. There are Native elders who raise their children in a Traditional way and warn them of Christians because if one becomes a Christian they will have to turn away from being Indian and become White. This is what Native people say to Christians. Because the past 500 years of evangelism has caused such trauma, Christians have a lot of work to do to make things right.

Missions is a 'dirty word' for First Nations people. It is almost as inappropriate *as assimilation or missionary*. First Nations people feel this way because they perceive evangelism as something that has been imposed on them. They also view missionaries with a large degree of distrust because they are discerned to be associated with the government (this is largely because of the Indians boarding schools and Residential schools were established by governments, while the day to day operation was fulfilled by the church), and are thought to be interested in one thing: land acquisition. For the purpose of this project the term 'Mission' is used to mean function, calling, or purpose rather than job or obligation.

Of course, there are also competent missionaries who, although they are exceptions to the rule, always endeavor to do their best and minister in a very caring and effective manner. However, one can spend too much time looking for 'the good guys' while hundreds of years of hurt are piled up on indigenous people. In order to feel better about one's faith and one's self, the overwhelming reality of the devastating effects of Christianity cannot be ignored.

The least favorite missionaries are those who know everything and believe that if only the people group (who are blessed to have them) would listen and carefully obey all that they say – the people would be saved. They impose their culture on the people rather than giving the gospel as a gift. They may as well be Conquistadors.

Preaching today needs to be contextualized. The reason preaching is so popular is because the precedent is biblically based. Whenever Jesus spoke He talked in parables, He taught, He was called Rabbi or Teacher. That was a format with which the people of His day were very familiar. Teachers were well received.

The revival preachers of the late 1800's in the United States and England were also warmly received. There was no television, radio, or any other form of communication beyond the written word. People found preachers interesting and wholeheartedly received them as well as their message.

Today a new context is needed for bringing the gospel to those to whom ministry is directed. Foursquare youth pastors and leaders readily acknowledge the need to contextualize ministry for young people and consequently they make giant strides in evangelizing and discipling youth. They use music, dance, story, games, and it is right and proper.

In the same way, a new model of ministry is needed to reach First Nations people. On the one hand, if there are Native people currently in non-Native style churches and they are satisfied, then let them stay. One does not have to teach Indians to be Indian. On the other hand, what is needed is direct attention to indigenous people who would never darken the doorway of a church because they were taught that the church was only interested in Indians for the purpose of assimilation and annihilation.

The Foursquare Church of today is not interested in assimilation; it is interested in leaving the gospel with the people, to be owned by them – that is proper missiology! Interestingly, the Foursquare church leads the fight when it comes to trusting indigenous leadership and giving First Nations leaders the power actually to assume control and make decisions for their own people.

Instead of doing church the way it has always been done, go to the powwow and find out what Creator is up to there. Indigenous instruments in church are needed in order to assist people to hear the gospel. One can hear many things when listening to the sound of a big drum and the voice of an ancient singer calling, The Creator made the trees, animals, and made it good. Creator gave humanity the creativity to fashion a drum out of elk hide and cedar bark, and gave him the unique sounding voices and chants. This is the voice of the one who Created us, Creator Jesus. He says Native people are as unique as any culture in the world.

Although Native people live on the land called the United States of America and Canada, they are a completely unique culture (hundreds of different cultures in fact) and need to be appropriately treated. Christian leaders will do well to remember that First Nations are a distinctive and beautiful people.

Proper Missiology calls for a *revolutionizing* of the way ministry is currently *done* to First Nations. Synonyms for the word 'doing' are such words as action, deed, undertaking, exploit, performance, achievement, accomplishment, and feat. These terms elicit extremely selfish reactions from a First Nations perspective. It must be asked, are these goals from God or from one's Self?

Who needs numbers and results to verify progress? More appropriate words for characterizing effective missionaries to indigenous people are serve, wait, support, encourage, relinquish control, yield to other cultural norms and ideas, mentor an indigenous person to take one's place as missionary, and then transfer to a new assignment.

Strong words? Yes, they are strong because most missionaries to indigenous people are seen as being involved in life-long endeavors whereas the goal should be to turn the work over to an indigenous leader.

It must be stated, however, that First Nations ministry is more daring than a simple weekend missions project – it is a life journey. Native people agree to journey together with their Native brothers and sisters toward the Creator who is revealed to them through Jesus Christ by the Holy Spirit. The author's mission for indigenous people is to determine what God was doing amongst them before she arrived on the scene.

The late well-known author and speaker Richard Twiss (Lakota Sioux) tells the story of an elder who was asked this question, 'Have you lived your whole life on the Reservation?' The elder answered, 'Not yet'. Not only does this exemplify the difference between Native and non-Native, it also illustrates how the journey is often more important than the destination.

The reason a revolution is needed in First Nations ministry is because there are *principles* in the mind of every non-Native pastor and leader within the Foursquare denomination in Canada and the United States that lead them to react a certain way toward First Nations people and First Nations ministry. These are philosophies, ideologies, and values about missiology to First Nations people that are not always accurate. Rather than reality, they sometimes rely upon pre-conceived ideas. There are also many stereotypes that non-Native people believe that, in fact, are absolutely false yet they need to be persuaded of the truth by Native people. The philosophies change with denominations but these are pressing issues that must be resolved and overcome in order for ministry to First Nations to be accurate in its presentation and thereby be effective. The Native people must own the gospel. This has never really happened in the life of the indigenous church of North America; they have never been fully trusted.

For the sake of unity '… I appeal to you, brothers, in the name of our Lord Jesus Christ, that all of you agree with one another so that there may be no divisions among you and that you may be perfectly united in mind and thought' (1 Cor. 1.10).

Should someone ask another to give up their culture for the sake of unity in the church? Indigenous people still hear these words today. Why? They hear these words because of the fear of the un-known. Many of the 'unknowns' in indigenous culture are very beautiful and have no religious significance whatsoever. However, most Native culture is judged on suspicion and the judgment is not based on any fact or even the slightest hint of knowledge.

Can one be American and also Christian? This question is al-most laughable because many people around the world equate American culture with being Christian.

> The reason Aboriginal Christians even have to wrestle with this issue of being Native and Christian is the result of this early and commonly accepted ethnocentric erroneous judgment. It is the same as asking a Canadian Christian, 'Can you be Canadian and Christian too?' Do we ask an American to give up being Ameri-can before becoming a Christian or in order to be a better one? These questions would be funny if it were not so pathetically applied to Aboriginal people.[70]

One cannot sweep cultural differences under the 'unity' carpet. Sometimes the Church can use unity like a weapon, believing that in order for there to be unity everything must be the same, which is not true unity. That is uniformity. Unity can only be achieved in the midst of diversity otherwise it is not unity but homogeneity.

The Scripture in 1 Cor 1.10 can be used as an anti-culture weap-on against people who are different. This Scripture can be twisted to make people conform to one's ideal of how a Christian should look, sound, act, sing, worship, and even smell. However, Paul was talking to the Corinthians about issues of the Spirit and not cultural differences, because the church in Corinth was Greek. 'He (Paul) and they (the Corinthian church community) are at odds on almost every issue; and their conflicting understandings of the Spirit and his activity seem to lie at the heart of things ... At issue throughout the letter, therefore, in most of its various parts, is a basic conflict over what it means to be people of the Spirit.'[71] Do not use this Scripture to defend one particular church culture style against an-other. There definitely are cultural issues within the context of Co-rinthians but all are within the Greek culture.

---

[70] Jacobs (Cayuga: Six Nations), *Aboriginal Christianity: The Way It Was Meant to Be*, p. 7.
[71] Fee, *Listening to the Spirit in the Text*, p. 83.

Contextualization is a missionary step that has all too often been overlooked. Try to think of a group of indigenous people who are Christians and have elements of culture within their churches. Because there are few pastors and leaders who will sit down and discuss Native traditions with Christian First Nations, there are few contextualized Native churches. Many First Nations people who have been acculturated do not believe they need to utilize Native instruments, songs, language, and culture within the church because they have grown so accustomed to the new church culture.

Ecclesiological Considerations

Common questions addressed to First Nations leaders by various other Christian leaders include: Why is it so hard to evangelize the First Nations? Why do Native people become Christians and then 'backslide' and return to their Indian religions?

Missionaries, pastors, and leaders ask these questions of Native people, and have been asking for many, many years. The answers usually target the Native people themselves – their lack of faith or their lack of commitment. Yet in reality, most of the blame lies in the methodology of the church itself. The church is largely irrelevant to the indigenous person because the church does not feel it needs to change in order to welcome a stranger, but rather expects that the stranger must just fit in. Every church has a culture and there are rules of engagement that are foreign to traditional indigenous people who have never previously darkened the doorway of a church.

Many Native people revert to their religions because they sense the presence of God in their ceremonies and they feel fully validated as an indigenous person. One of the effects of colonization has been the identity struggle experienced by many indigenous people. While there is a strong tie to the past, to culture, and to traditions, there is also an identity crisis within every indigenous person. 'Whether an Indian person can be at peace with himself can only be answered by each individual As an Ojibwa counselor at Northern Arizona University observed, "Every Indian person I know has an identity issue".'[72]

---

[72] Champagne (ed.), *Contemporary Native American Cultural Issues*, p. 29.

Perhaps Native people are more sensory and enjoy the ceremony where they feel something happens on a level that they understand. Christians experience this in church but again, church culture is largely foreign to indigenous people.

Many Christians feel skeptical about Native traditions. If Christians are apprehensive about something, they will withdraw. There are dozens of questions that Native people are forced to answer about their culture and sometimes it can get tiring. Imagine if someone from another culture was constantly questioning American culture and portraying it as scary and ungodly. A good comparison is when some Muslims call Americans infidels.[73] These words draw boundaries, divide, and intimidate.

While many Native people continue to answer the questions, some simply withdraw themselves from the prying questions, the inquisitive stares, and the disapproving glance in their direction. Remember, people are ethnocentric. People tend to like that to which they are accustomed, and if anybody trifles with their stable lives, they get upset.

That is unfortunate because Native people do not need validation from the church to feel Native or to be accepted by the church. They will just leave. That is exactly what the Enemy of the soul desires, to create division and cause trouble. There should be unity in the body of Christ and First Nations should be accepted as they are.

In answer to the question, why do Native people 'backslide' or go back to their own ways, it is because Christianity has never been incarnated into the worldview of the indigenous person. It is never even attempted. When a Native person enters a church, the pastor and people are just happy to have another body. They do not recognize that Native people need something more – because a huge chunk of their heart (their very identity) is left out of the church. This is not true for Native people who have been Christians for a long time, or if Christianity has been in their family for generations. These Native people are already acculturated into the dominant church culture.

---

[73] Infidel: (1) Unbeliever: Somebody who does not believe in a major religion, especially Christianity or Islam; (2) Nonbeliever: Somebody with no religious belief. Encarta Dictionary: English, 2008.

Neither the early missionaries nor the modern missionaries have successfully placed the gospel into the hands of the First Nations people and *trusted* them with it. Today, First Nations are still seen a mission field even though it has been 500 years since 'discovery'. Sadly, First Nations continue to think that Christianity is inextricably tied to the 'White Man's Culture' and therefore is his gospel.

Native people have not wholly accepted the Christian faith because their faith has not wholly touched their Indian soul. They want to see a revival among their people starting from the inside out; that God would heal the shattered self-esteem of their people and reveal that He is not a God who is against them but who created and loves them.

How do white Americans or Canadians perceive Jesus' death? Jesus is perceived as sacrificial giving his life so that man might live and that is correct.

How would the death of Jesus be perceived by the vast majority of Jews at the time? They saw it as the most shameful way to die. To the Jews, Jesus died a failure. Jesus' followers were looking for an insurrectionist to overthrown the oppressive Roman government. When Jesus died, their dream of displacing the oppressive, dominant Roman culture also died.

One does not hear or understand this story today because they are living in countries that are perceived as the greatest places in the world to live. American culture daily is exported via the Internet, television, and satellite to an envious or resentful world. Americans and Canadians cannot relate to Jesus' followers who scattered that day, fearing arrest and trial as insurrectionists, because today they are part of a dominant culture. However, Jesus' resurrection was the greatest insurrection of all, it was not an assault against a culture or people but against death itself. Self-resurrection proved divinity.

To understand the context of the Biblical narrative, Pastors and leaders must learn the basics of Jewish culture. Without the context any interpretation can be applied to the content. The culture gives meaning to man and reveals God to him.

For many Native people, the Bible is interpreted by white people through their white culture. In Sunday school, a felt Jesus and his felt disciples are always white with shiny blond hair.

The best way to preach a sermon is to select a Bible story and re-contextualize it for the particular audience. Every minister contextualizes their message before they preach. If they are speaking to female inmates, to a youth group, or to a newlywed's home group, they will appropriate a suitable sermon for the setting.

A First Nations Identity

Because of the ill-adapted Missiology applied to First Nations at their 'discovery', their culture, language, and traditions were rejected and replaced by European culture, language, and traditions. Philosophically, this gave good reason to question whether or not it was acceptable even to be Native. Because of this, many First Nations feel shame in their identity. It is not cool to be Native. Many indigenous people deeply resent those who attacked them physiologically and sociologically and have become firmer in their resolve to reject Christianity.

One's ethnicity seems to give others the right to regard one with suspicion and cynicism. Somewhere along the journey, self-respect and dignity were lost and First Nations could not take pride in their heritage.

One focused glance at correct Missiology will cause the reevaluation of one's stance towards ministry to First Nations. Missiology to First Nations people needs to be conducted as one would in other foreign mission fields, including conformance to proper protocol.

Common thinking often is, 'Why can't Native people just be like us?' or 'They live in Canada and America where everyone is equal so they should not expect special treatment'. Those statements sound ethnocentric at best and racist at worst. While it is true that Native people do not desire or expect 'special' treatment, they do expect to be recognized as a different culture.

The Need for a Unique First Nations Church

First Nations of North, Central, and South America were given the gospel and thank God for it. However, it was not presented in a godly manner. Families were separated and told it was better to become like someone else (put on a European costume) in order to be accepted by God. This falsehood has passed through generation after generation until now. There is something new stirring in the hearts of First Nations believers. One can receive Christ as an incarnated Indian and worship Him. Jesus walks right up to one and begins to get to the heart of their troubles.

Conclusion

This chapter on theological foundations brings clarity to the indigenous view of God. Indigenous people have always respected Creator and have a high regard for spirituality and prayer. If Christians can walk alongside indigenous people, learning their culture and customs, and then gradually introduce an understanding of the Holy Spirit and Jesus, those Christians will have success in their missionary efforts.

The Old Testament tells of how other nations of the world evidence faith. This faith is acknowledged by God in Mal. 1.11, 'My name will be great among the nations from the rising from the setting of the sun. In every place incense and pure offerings will be brought to my name, because my name will be great among the nations, says the Lord Almighty.' *The Message* version of the Bible says it quite beautifully: 'I am honored all over the world. And there are people who know how to worship me all over the world, who honor me by bringing their best to me'.[74]

First Nations beliefs are similar to an Old Testament understanding of God and if they can learn to walk alongside they will do a great justice to this Good News they bear.

Anthropologists give logical warnings to those interested in learning about other cultures. While one is learning about the culture, he or she should not immediately correct what is theologically wrong with the culture or the conversation will end. The challenge for the anthropologist is to describe accurately the people as they see themselves, not to make a judgment call on the soundness of their theology. This posture should be that which is assumed by missionaries as well. Adopting this stance will result in trust being instilled in the local people, which is the most overlooked and yet necessary element in missions work. By and large, most indigenous people embrace moral codes, societal rules, spiritual beliefs, and stories. Is there anything wrong with walking alongside a people group for a season, learning from them, getting to know them, and being humble?

Indigenous people recognize God as the Creator, Great Spirit, or Grandfather. The Holy Spirit is understood as a presence exist-

---

[74] Peterson, *The Messsage*.

ent in nature while Jesus is found in a few prophecies. Bringing the clarity expressed below to indigenous people is practicing proper Missiology,

> I happened upon a Native man whose artwork included spiritual pictures. He had a picture of nail pierced hands but said he was not a Christian. I began to tell him how Christians thought of Creator, that Creator came down in the form of a man, primarily to show the way to Creator, but also that this one might know the suffering of humanity. The Native man said, 'No one ever told me that before'.[75]

The section on Land Theology explains why indigenous people believe the earth is infused with the Spirit, and unfortunately sometimes this can lead to erroneous conclusions. However, First Nations are much closer to understanding the Biblical truths than perhaps a dyed-in-the-wool atheistic scientist. Indigenous people also are very much connected to the land because of the Divine Placement stories, which inherently give Native people a continued responsibility to steward the land.

The Missiology section is one of the most important sections in this project. Recognition that indigenous people are from completely different cultures is critical; only then can conventional missiological procedures be introduced into the ministry. These fundamental steps have often been overlooked and misunderstood when ministering to First Nations in Canada and the United States.

The Ecclesiology section provides the guidelines for an indigenous Church and the need for missiology to extend as well to the indigenous church.

---

[75] Memories on the Powwow Trail by Cheryl Bear-Barnetson, Journal July 2007.

3

THEOLOGICAL INTEGRATION

Introduction

The purpose of this chapter is to discover what Native and non-Native writers disclose concerning ministry to indigenous people with regard to theology, missiology, anthropology, indigenous worldview, and stereotypes and to integrate those views with the claims made in Chapter 2. It will provide convincing evidence that First Nations are unique but that many of the indigenous beliefs and traditions have theological correspondence to the broader Christian tradition and are deserving of respect. Part One will outline the indigenous worldview while Part Two focuses on theology.

This review will begin with a critique of Oral Tradition, which is a valid and recognized form of historical recording.

A theological section will consider the thoughts of Native theologians, pastors, and leaders from across Canada and the United States.

A missiological component will include thoughts from Sherwood G. Lingenfelter and Marvin K. Mayers through their book, *Ministering Cross-Culturally: An Incarnational Model for Personal Relationships*. This section will also provide an overview of Paul's missionary concepts found in Acts with a simple but succinct read-through of the book of Acts.

Finally, a First Nations component will present quotes from Hugo Miller's crucial book, *Why Don't You?: A look at Attitudes towards Indians*, and will provide amply study for non-Native perceptions of indigenous people. A commentary on stereotypes is included and is based on an overview of a book by Devon A. Mihesuah, *American Indians: Stereotypes and Realities*.

Part One – Indigenous Worldview

Indigenous History – Oral Tradition

There are innumerable books written about the indigenous people in Canada and the United States, with some being more accurate than others. Native people have a different view of history. One cannot allow their historical memories to collapse into western history, which has Columbus founding the Americas. 'If this amnesiac view of North American history is to change, then one must first revive the memories of people lying hidden within one's self, for one is the same yet different from one's ancestors.'[1]

> Ours is not only a history of oppression. No, it is the history of peoples who lived at least 13,000 years on this continent, by modest estimates, before Columbus arrived. Our people created cultures based upon spiritual beliefs which bound them together in a life of simplicity and balance with each other and with the earth. These cultures were never static; they adapted and changed according to the needs of survival and spirit.

> Theirs was not a life of perfection. We do not mean to remember our ancestors as though they were all saints or 'noble savages' living in paradise. They were prone to error as all humans yet they, like many indigenous people of the earth, founded and lived a balanced way of life. Many of them became persons of great character and dignity.

> Recall the Arawak people who swam out and went in boats to welcome Columbus and his strange entourage as he sailed into their home waters. There is irony in this story of hospitality, for the Arawak unknowingly welcomed their own destruction.[2]

Another reason the history is not accurate is that it does not include the perspective of the indigenous people themselves. This is troubling to indigenous people because non-Natives are writing

---

[1] Treat (ed.), *Native and Christian*, p. 134.
[2] Treat (ed.), *Native and Christian*, p. 134.

their own perspective into their account of Native people. Various Native authors, from many different Native Nations who have decided it is time to set the record straight, are alleviating this problem. This chapter will utilize many Native authors to drive home one of the central themes of this project: Indigenous people in Canada and the United States are different from everyone else and must be taken into special consideration especially when a church desires to reach out and minister to indigenous people.

Devon Mihesuah (Choctaw), in her book *Natives and Academics: Researching and Writing about American Indians*, sheds some light on the situation,

> … works on American Indian history and culture should not give only one perspective; the analyses must include Indians' versions of events. Many authors of books hailed as the 'New Indian History,' however, have never consulted tribal people for information. Referring to the problem, Angela Cavender Wilson writes in her first essay, 'American Indian History or Non-Indian perceptions of American Indian History?' that this type of work is not really American Indian history; rather, it is Indian history interpreted by non-Indians and should be labeled as such.[3]

Oral tradition is one of the troubling issues non-Native historians encounter with history from a First Nations perspective is oral tradition. They deem it unreliable. 'Many historians and anthropologists also argue that Indians cannot accurately recount their past using oral traditions. They refuse to use informants, believing modern Indians' versions of their tribes' histories are "fantasies".'[4] However, the Pentateuch is based on oral tradition[5] as well as the Gospels of Mark[6] and Luke[7] in the New Testament. Christians have a lot anchored on the truth of oral tradition.

---

[3] Devon A. Mihesuah, *Natives and Academics: Researching and Writing about American Indians* (Lincoln, NE: University of Nebraska Press, 1998), p. 1.

[4] Mihesuah, *Natives and Academics*, p. 2.

[5] The events of Creation happened thousands of years before the author of Genesis was born. He was not there for these events and therefore relied upon Oral Tradition.

[6] Mark was not one of the original disciples and thereby relied on Oral Tradition.

[7] Luke reveals this himself in Lk. 1.1-4.

Many have undertaken to draw up an account of the things that have been fulfilled among us, just as they were handed down to us by those who from the first were eyewitnesses and servants of the word. Therefore, since I myself have carefully investigated everything from the beginning, it seemed good also to me to write an orderly account for you, most excellent Theophilus, so that you may know the certainty of the things you have been taught (Lk. 1.1-4).

One of the reasons that the oral history of indigenous peoples is not taken into consideration is lack of trust. Unfortunately, there is an ongoing issue of trust between indigenous and non-Native people that has never been overcome either by the church when it comes to the gospel, or the government when it comes to indigenous self-government. This has changed to a certain degree within certain denominations including Foursquare Canada and the United States. Further discussion on this subject is found in Chapter Six. George E. Tinker (Osage/Cherokee) writes in his carefully researched work:

> What becomes consistently apparent is that missionaries of all denominations could not trust American Indian converts with the gospel of Jesus Christ. Instead, fearing a reversion to old cultural habits, they constantly policed their converts, rooting out suspicious behaviors. Disciplinary control, the imposition of European culture, and even the imposition of European economic structures and technology actually became the gospel, even though it was necessarily a gospel of bondage rather than one of liberation.[8]

That huge barrier needs to be overcome if there is to be any development in the relationship between Natives and non-Natives. This is an issue when it comes to entrusting indigenous leaders with church governance and at the local church level when raising up and entrusting a Native leader in the church to be a minister. Some churches do very well in dealing with these subjects, and it seems that the Foursquare Church in the United States and Canada is on the right track, but much remains to be accomplished.

---

[8] George E. Tinker, *Missionary Conquest: The Gospel and Native American Cultural Genocide* (Minneapolis: Fortress Press, 1993), p. 20.

The reasons Native leaders are not relied upon are often based on stereotype, assumption, and perhaps a little 'but we've never done that before!'

This is not uncommon because of the stereotypes that have plagued First Nation people since the first meeting with Europeans. These misconceptions and prejudices continue today. However, the idea of the cultural genocide of indigenous nations has been percolating for a number of years.

Stereotypes

The old West conjures up a wide variety of images in the modern mind. Memories of John Wayne movies, Roy Rogers, The Lone Ranger and Tonto all fighting bad White guys and bad Indians.

> We also have images of the Native relationship with white America: the first 'Thanksgiving,' the Little Big Horn, Wounded Knee, leaders like Chief Joseph and Sitting Bull, and, yes, even John Wayne movies. Such images whether veridical or dangerously mythological and even racist – of these two facts of the Native American experience almost exhaust the non-Indian's conception of all that is Indian. For many non-Indians, the Indian is a two-dimensional cartoon. What is missing, or at best uncommon, is a third kind of image: that of Native American relationships with each other. While there are a few icons such as the 'chief,' the 'squaw,' the 'papoose,' and the 'brave,' there is a paucity of images – real or imagined – of activity and attitudes within the community.[9]

'One of the few Westerns on the radio was the famous Lone Ranger with his steady but stereotypical Indian companion, Tonto, which means *fool* in Spanish.'[10] Spanish speaking people often wondered why the Lone Ranger's Indian sidekick was given such a name. Misunderstanding has been the rule when Canadians and American consider the indigenous people. This not only affects average citizens but also is reflected in the statement of political leaders:

---

[9] Champagne (ed.), *Contemporary Native American Cultural Issues*, pp. 277-92.
[10] Berkhofer, *The White Man's Indian*, p. 102.

Ronald Reagan's statement in 1988 that 'maybe we should not have humored Indians in their primitive lifestyle – maybe they should have been made citizens like everyone else',[11] proves that ignorance about Indian history still thrives in our society. Some people – people with political power – still regard the concepts of termination and ethnocide as viable despite the struggles of Native Americans for their rights.[12]

This section will cover a few of many stereotypes of indigenous peoples. Westerners have stereotyped Native people to the point that Indians exist only as bizarre, fantastical caricatures either of the docile elder or the bloodthirsty warrior.[13]

> Until the occupation of Wounded Knee American Indians were stereotyped in literature and by the media. They were either a villainous warlike group that lurked in the darkness thirsting for blood of innocent settlers or the calm, wise, dignified elder sitting on the mesa dispensing his wisdom in poetic aphorisms.[14]

There were, of course, Indian wars with settlers and the army. One can simply say a few words to bring back the memory of the Battle of Greasy Grass[15] and Batoche.[16] However, these Indian wars do not compare with the cruelties Indians have suffered at the hand of the government and the church after the wars ended. Native people were never conquered because of inferiority but rather because of their lack of immunity to European diseases.[17] That would not make a very good western, with Native riders flying off their horses because John Wayne sneezed on them, which however, is closer to the truth.

---

[11] The author, Rachel L. Spieldoch footnotes this, 'President Ronald Reagan made this statement during his 1988 visit to the former Soviet Union' (*Frontline*, Boston, WGBH, 58 min., 1988).

[12] Champagne (ed.), *Contemporary Native American Cultural Issues*, p. 315.

[13] Mihesuah, *American Indians: Stereotypes and Realities*, p. 48.

[14] Vine Deloria, Jr. (Yankton Sioux), *God is Red* (New York: Dell Publishing, 1973), p. 23.

[15] The Native people called the Little Big Horn hill Greasy Grass because it was very slippery.

[16] Batoche, Saskatchewan in 1885.

[17] Mihesuah, *American Indians: Stereotypes and Realities*, p. 29.

The first century after contact was the most disastrous; between 1520 and 1600, 31 major epidemics swept across the Atlantic Coast from South America to Canada. So devastating were these epidemics that the Indian population of North America fell from 7 million at contact to 3 million individuals within 100 years, while still greater losses in overall number occurred in the heavily populated regions of Mexico and South America, especially Peru. Europeans quickly learned of Indians' susceptibility to disease, and in 1763 British Officers led by Lord Jeffrey Amherst (a college and numerous towns have been christened with his name) sent blankets infected with smallpox to Ottawas and other tribes in an attempt to quell Pontiac's uprising.[18]

However, one did not see the last of the diseases. In 1910 there was another epidemic that wiped out many more indigenous people. In the author's grandmother's village there were mass graves because those left behind were themselves too weak and sick to provide proper burial. The mass grave is still there today. The author's grandfather, before marrying my grandmother, was married and had five children who all died of germs that today can be alleviated by over-the-counter medicine. However, today there are still epidemics occurring and it seems that other battles are being lost, not against small pox but against tuberculosis and diabetes. Before contact with Europeans, Native people did not have diabetes because of their nutritional diets but today more than half the Native population suffers from diabetes. No one caricatures the old west with thousands upon thousands of dead, decaying bodies killed by germ warfare.

To many Christians of that day, the mass epidemics that wiped out many Native people were understood to be God's will. God eradicated all the Indians so that Europeans could take the land and settle here, thereby removing (some of them) from religious persecution in England. They then turned out to be the major contributors of religious persecution to Native people in the 'New' World. Manifest Destiny is based on the Old Testament where God led Abraham and later Moses to take their new land from the heathens. There is no room here to discuss the malicious and devious meth-

---

[18] Mihesuah, *American Indians: Stereotypes and Realities*, p. 29.

ods used in signing treaties. Even the strongest tribes[19] were suppressed when their main source of food was 'systematically destroyed by hide hunting promoted by those who believed the death of the bison would mean death to the Indians'.[20]

It is no wonder that certain indigenous people are very angry at the church. One Christian Native brother became very angry when he read Dee Brown's historical account in his book, *Bury My Heart At Wounded Knee*, because it details the great injustices perpetrated.

> For now, some generalizations can be made to characterize the frontier myth as a distinct way of representing history. First, history is understood as the heroic struggle between the forces of good and evil, where conflict and violence are naturalized and seen as the very motor that drives history. The frontier myth is drawn upon not only to provide an explanation of history and of contemporary social and political arrangements, but also to provide a metaphysical understanding of the nature of history, individual agency, and humankind's ongoing relationship to the social and natural world.[21]

Native people still consider themselves warriors. The fight continues for their land, their people, their resources, and even for the country. At every powwow veterans lead the Grand Entry. The Grand Entry marks the beginning of the powwow when the flags (usually of America, Canada, and the Native flag, which is also called a buffalo staff) are brought in carried by veterans and followed by every dancer in full regalia. Veterans are highly honored at the powwows and by the Native people everywhere. When a speech is given they will usually begin by acknowledging Chiefs, Elders, and Veterans. This may surprise some,

> Indians have fought for the United States in every single war this country (or its colonists) have been involved in (though of course many Indians fought against the American colonists during the colonial period), the War of 1812, and the Civil War. More recently, 8,000 Indians fought in World War I; 25,000 fought in World War II and representatives of several tribes,

---

[19] Such as the Sioux who defeated Custer at Greasy Grass.

[20] Mihesuah, *American Indians: Stereotypes and Realities*, p. 30.

[21] Cited by Furniss, 'Pioneers, Progress, and the Myth of the Frontier, p. 10.

most notably Navajos, Choctaws. Comanches, and some Apaches, served as Code Talkers; 41,000 Indians served in Vietnam, and 24,000 served in Operation Desert Storm.[22]

Unfortunately, indigenous people are more often employed to represent all that was evil against the forces of good and the press of progress such as in the old westerns. The stereotypes continue because the movies are still playing. No one questions the mighty hero John Wayne. However, some of the worst stereotypes were directed toward indigenous women.

> Because of the influence of television, movies and literature, non-Indian Americans usually think of Indian women in either of two contradictory ways: 1) they are ugly, dirty, subservient, abused 'squaws' who loved to torture white men; or 2) they are beautiful, exotic 'Princesses,' often Chief's daughters, usually willing to leave their people to marry dashing Europeans.[23]

There are modern day stereotypes of Native women that are even more distasteful. Indigenous girls are seen as easy marks and continue to be preyed upon by males. There are many missing women along the 'Highway of Tears' in northern British Columbia and most of them are Native. Unfortunately, most of these cases are cold.

Another common stereotype is that all Native people are the same.[24] There are, however, approximately 1,000 different nations in Canada, and the United States, and Mexico. Believing that all Native Nations are the same is like saying a British person is the same as a German, that a Kiwi is the same as an Australian. These statements not only are untrue, they are grossly inflammatory (just ask members of any of the above nationalities if they appreciate being compared to the other!)

There are hundreds and hundreds of languages, customs, cultures, and practices. Each tribal group has a similar history and affinity with other nations but retains a distinct uniqueness. In order to minister to a particular Nation, one must become a student of that people and first learn a few things.

---

[22] Mihesuah, *American Indians: Stereotypes and Realities*, p. 55.

[23] Mihesuah, *American Indians: Stereotypes and Realities*, p. 61.

[24] Mihesuah, *American Indians: Stereotypes and Realities*, pp. 20-28.

Most non-Native people either are not aware that there are ancient Native villages in close proximity to their homes and cities or
they know about the Reservation but do not know what to think
about it. If they happen to drive through a Native Reservation or
village, they do not remember history and simply feel pity for the
poor, dilapidated homes, and likely drunken Indians. Sometimes
non-Native people wonder if Native people are still imprisoned on
their Reservations as was historically the case. These are common
perceptions and stereotypes of First Nations people. However, the
stereotype of Natives being imprisoned by their Reserves is quite
ridiculous, but one would be surprised at how many questions on
this subject indigenous people have to answer.

First Nations are not imprisoned on their land. These stereotypes are based on historical facts that today no longer exist. Native
people are proud to have fought for and to retain land rights. Formerly in the United States, the reservation in particular felt like a
prison but now it has become the only land they have and it has
become home.

Native people see their 'tribes' as sovereign Nations and there
are hundreds of sovereign Nations living within the confines of the
Canadian and the American borders.

There are many other stereotypes of First Nations people. The
drunk is the most common,[25] and unfortunately Native people tend
to have all the problems associated with alcohol. Native people
have a high degree of alcohol abuse. This can be traced to depres-
sion from the effects of colonization and not a propensity for alcohol abuse.

> The most persistent myth about Indians is that they have a par-
> ticular biophysical reason for 'not being able to hold their alco-
> hol.' In fact, not only do non-Indians believe this, but many In-
> dians also believe that their entire group has a biological deficit
> in metabolizing alcohol ... no basis at all for this myth is found
> in the scientific literature, and it should not be a consideration in
> current prevention and intervention programs. Major reviews of
> alcohol metabolism among all ethnic groups usually conclude
> that there is more variation within an ethnic group than there is
> between ethnic groups. Further, when bio-physiologic investiga-

[25] Mihesuah, *American Indians: Stereotypes and Realities*, pp. 97-98.

tors attempt to explain major alcohol-related behaviors, they generally point to socio-cultural variables as the major factors.[26]

There are severe issues that accompany drinking to which Native people fall victim. These statistics are shocking:

Recent HIS data indicate that Indians die more frequently than the U.S. averages from motor vehicle accidents (2.95 to 3.89 times higher); other accidents (2.99 to 4.05 times higher); suicide (1.53 to 1.95 times higher); homicide (1.97 to 2.34 times higher); and alcoholism (5.45 to 7.63 times higher). These ratios of Indian to U.S. averages reflect rates, not the actual number of deaths. There are three elements of explanation for this different experience. One element can be found in the previous sections, which deal with demographic, social and political considerations discussed in the literature. The second element of explanation is centered on drinking style. The flamboyant drinking styles that are very common in a number of Indian peer clusters (recreational and anxiety drinkers) emphasize abusive drinking and high blood alcohol levels. Further, heavy drinking peer groups among many tribes encourage, or do not discourage, the frequent mixing of alcohol impairment, risky behavior, and risky environments. Driving while intoxicated, sleeping outside in the winter, aggression, and other unsafe practices are examples of this element.[27]

Many people believe alcohol abuse starts as a choice and then leads to alcoholism, which is a symptom of coping with pain. The pain that indigenous people have suffered is truly great. There is no amount of medication that can heal the open, infected wounds from the historical past, except the One who is Good Medicine: Jesus is the only medicine that can heal the Ancient Wounds.

Then there are the mascots, found mostly in the United States, which really bother indigenous people. Picture in one's mind the mascot of the Cleveland Indians baseball team.[28] Everyone can easi-

---

[26] Champagne (ed.), *Contemporary Native American Cultural Issues*, p. 229.

[27] Champagne (ed.), *Contemporary Native American Cultural Issues*, p. 233.

[28] Unfortunately, it does not stop in the major leagues, many local American Elementary, Jr. High and High Schools have Indian mascots even though Native people petition and protest against them.

ly conjure up this image because of the team's marketing strategies. Apparently, no one thinks having *Indians* as mascots is a problem. However, no one would ever call their team the Cleveland Blacks, the Cleveland Jews, or the Cleveland Whities. If they did, they would be branded racist in front of the entire Nation, made to apologize, throw away anything resembling the racist mascot, and start from scratch. Indigenous people are always protesting Native mascots but no one ever hears about it, mostly because the team owners believe they are somehow bringing honor to the 'spirit' of the Indian people or perhaps they know Indians make for good marketing. Their excuses do not matter. To indigenous people this is racist.

There are other misconceptions about indigenous people as well. This one is recurring: 'Why can't they just get a job?' The stereotypical lazy Indian is another:

> The whites believe that there is a great danger the lazy Indian will eventually corrupt God's hardworking people. He is still suspicious that the Indian way of life is dreadfully wrong. There is, in fact, something un-American about Indians for most whites.[29]

Different values of indigenous people have been examined but the one that will be discussed here is work, because it falls into the stereotyping section. Indigenous people value work (to think otherwise is laughable), but hold work in its proper perspective – as work, not life. Certain Native people pursue careers and yet still do not hold the career over and above family. Most indigenous people will *not* keep a job that interferes with their cultural and familial duties. There are funerals, weddings, potlatches, powwows, birthdays, christenings, and all are expected to attend. However, when traveling from one city to another proves to take more time than the job allows, the Native person will often get into trouble. This does not reveal a lack of respect for work or the employer, but rather a holistic lifestyle that revolves around family and culture. The lifestyle is based on the cycles of nature. There is no salmon run in the winter so the people do not fish until summer. They follow the rhythms of

---

[29] Vine Deloria, Jr. (Yankton Sioux), *Custer Died For Your Sins: An Indian Manifesto* (New York: The Macmillan Company, 1969), p. 4.

nature in their lifestyle and work habits and continue to do so. In villages along the West coast of British Columbia due to the salmon run, August is a very busy month. Years ago there would be twenty-four hour workdays lasting for three or four days until all the fish were cleaned. Fishermen are accustomed to working in these conditions for months.

Indians in northern Canada are well-known for their ability to persist, though work is arduous and the weather dangerously cold; white people often say no one can out-work them. This demonstrates that Native people are seasonal workers and place life, family, and work in their proper perspective. Not every boss will commend one's dedicated parenting, nor their devotion to mother and father. Many times the Native people lose their jobs because of their schedules.

This mind-set also affects post-secondary education. Many Native students find the schedules taxing because they are on a strict semester system that does not allow for more than a few absences. When students are needed back home it conflicts with their schooling. The entire post-secondary education system is structured to accommodate students who will attend for many years. Another detrimental consequence of the school system is that many students leave their Reservation to attend and return home with their thought processes having been changed; or worse, they do not come home at all but grow accustomed to city life. If they had been able to study in their own environment, they would be able to maintain their traditions and cultures. Also, when students decide to live in the city for whatever reason, the village, as well as the individuals, suffers the consequences.

Today, many online studies are available that benefit Native people who do not desire to leave their villages. For example, www.fnbc.org is an online two-year program, which upon completion will allow a First Nations person to begin the licensing process with Foursquare Canada together with a number of transferable credits. Built on a module system, the two years cover all the doctrinal courses with an emphasis on First Nations perspective.

The last straw for most indigenous people is when White people play Indian. Indigenous means inherently from some country, natural or inborn.[30] First Nations are from North America and everyone else is an immigrant. Immigrants struggled to make themselves at home here and began playing Indian in order to feel indigenous.

Philip J. Deloria in his seminal work, *Playing Indian,* argues that since the Boston Tea Party, Americans have played Indian by creating a new American identity. The only way immigrants felt indigenous was to pretend to be indigenous. He includes a large section on the Boy Scout movement in America (which also affected Canada). Boy Scouts presented an erroneous perception of indigenous people to the United States and Canada. Prevalent stereotypes are partially derived from these times.

> Indianness has, above all, represented identities that are unquestionably American. Despite the shifting nature of individual, social, and national identities, Indianness has made them seem fixed and final. For the Tea Party Indians and Tammany paraders of the Revolution, aboriginal Indianness made one a citizen, not of an impermanent government, but of the land itself. That half-secret meaning, as D.H. Lawrence half-realized was as powerful as the timeless earth was real. For those who came here from other countries, the ultimate truths of America's physical nature – rocks, water, sky – were intimately linked to a meta-physical[31] American nature that would always be bound up with mythic national identities. The secrets of both natures lay in Indianness.[32]

Deloria discusses postmodernism and how it came from Americans playing Indian during the 1960's and 1970's. American and Canadians embraced Native philosophy, tied it to Eastern beliefs, conjuring up the New Age movement and resulting in discontentment with modernity. In the quote below Philip J. Deloria tells of how, although playing Indian shaped American identity, it has not been in the best interest of the indigenous people.

---

[30] Microsoft Encarta Encyclopedia, 2008.

[31] The different font here and in the next quote is replicated from the book itself.

[32] Phillip J. Deloria (Yankton Sioux), *Playing Indian* (New Haven, CT: Yale University Press, 1998), p. 183.

Playing Indian reflects one final paradox. The self-defining pairing of American truths with American freedom rests on the ability to wield power against Indians – social, military, economic, and political – while simultaneously drawing power from the Indianness may have existed primarily as a cultural artifact in American society, but it has helped create these other forms of power, which have then been turned back on Native people. The dispossessing of Indians exists in tension with being aboriginally true. The embracing of Indians exists in equal tension with the freedom to become new. And the terms are interchangeable. Intricate relations between destruction and creativity – for both Indians and non-Indian Americans – are themselves suspended in an uneasy alliance. And so while Indian people have lived out a collection of historical nightmares in the material world, they have also haunted a long night of American dreams. As many native people have observed, to be American is to be unfinished. And although that state is powerful and creative, it carries with it nightmares all its own.[33]

The stereotypes section will be concluded here. There are many more books and quotes that could be referenced but the preceding pages provide a clear synopsis of the subject. First Nation people are some of the most misunderstood people.

The task of understanding an indigenous point of view is paramount to beginning any First Nations ministry. Without the proper insight, ministry to a people will be ineffective. It has historically been shown that lack of knowledge of one's subject can only lead to tragedy, disillusionment, and failure.

Part Two: Theology

Gregory of Nyssa – The Cloud of Unknowing

This section will demonstrate how the early church father Gregory of Nyssa relates to an indigenous understanding of Creator. The care and beauty in the way indigenous people talk about Creator is similar to that of Gregory, someone who is a celebrated early Christian theologian. To learn about his philosophy of prayer in seeking

---

[33] Deloria (Yankton Sioux), *Playing Indian*, p. 191.

the Unknown God is truly refreshing and illuminates some of the same First Nations thoughts regarding the Transcendence of God.

Gregory of Nyssa, *ca* 335-*ca* 394 CE, was a, 'champion of Nicene orthodoxy',[34] and one of the Cappadocian Fathers who developed 'apophatic theology' or 'negative theology'.[35] 'Theodosius I named (Gregory) a standard of orthodoxy and touchstone of ecclesiastical fellowship in Pontus.'[36] He was also a Father of Orthodoxy, was very familiar with Christian doctrine, and defended the faith against limited incarnation.[37] Gregory of Nyssa had a solid grasp of the Scriptures, teaching, doctrine, and theology. He also professed the theology closest to indigenous thought and philosophy of the Creator. Gregory of Nyssa's approach to God is very similar to that of indigenous people.

In, *Moses: The servant of the Lord,*[38] Gregory explains the impassability of God. To say, 'I want to see God', is to say that God is knowable and understood when He is infinite and unknowable. Is one's search for a knowable God made real only when one makes God in one's own image? A poem by C.S. Lewis illuminates how people create God in their own image using anthropomorphisms. Anthropomorphisms use human language to describe God, for example, talking about the 'hand of the Lord'[39] helps one to understand God in human terms. However, it does not help people to seek the Unknown. The poem by C.S. Lewis illustrates this beautifully,

> Our arrow, aimed unskillfully, beyond desert;
> and all men are idolaters, crying unheard
> To a deaf idol, if Thou take them at their word.[40]

---

[34] Robert Atwell (ed.), *Gregory of Nyssa: Spiritual Classics from the Early Church* (London: Church House, 1995). *Gregory of Nyssa: In the Shadow of His Glory*, p. 87.

[35] Atwell (ed.), *Gregory of Nyssa*, p. 88.

[36] Elwell, *Evangelical Dictionary of Theology*, p. 487.

[37] Elwell, *Evangelical Dictionary of Theology*, p 487. 'Against Apollinaris he argues for a full incarnation in the treatise *Antirrheticus*'.

[38] Atwell (ed.), *Gregory of Nyssa*, p. 87.

[39] For example, the phrase 'the hand of the Lord' is in the Bible 22 times. Exod. 9.3; Josh. 4.24; Judg. 2.15; 1 Sam. 7.13; 1 Kgs 18.46; 2 Kgs 3.15; 1 Chron. 28.19; Ezra 7.6, 28; Job 12.9; Ps. 75.8; Prov. 21.1; Isa. 25.10, 41.20, 51.17, 66.14; Ezek. 1.3; 3.14, 22, 33.22; 37.1; 40.1, Acts 11.21; 13.11.

[40] Cited by Walter Harper (ed.), *Poems* (New York: Harcourt Ball, 1964), p. 85.

Gregory of Nyssa believed people create an idol, even when they use their best language to describe God.[41] He encouraged people not to use any language or symbolism in their meditations of God because they would distract themselves from the truth about God. This is true of many First Nations who believe that Creator is a Spirit. They are not theologically incorrect but why not walk further with them in their understanding before laying on them what might be perceived as sanctimonious knowledge.

The Native view that creation is a better cathedral than humans can produce sounds like Paul talking to the Athenians in Acts. Consider these words from Ohiyesa, Charles Eastman (Wahpeton Dakota):

> There were no temples or shrines among us save those of nature. Being a natural man, the Indian was intensely poetical. He would deem it sacrilege to build a house for Him who may be met face to face in the mysterious, shadowy aisle of the primeval forest, or on the sunlit bosom of virgin prairies, upon dizzy spires and pinnacles of naked rock, and yonder in the jeweled vault of the night sky! He who enrobes Himself in filmy veils of cloud, there on the rim of the visible world where our Great-grandfather Sun kindles his evening campfire; He who rides upon the rigorous wind of the north, or breathes forth His spirit upon aromatic southern airs, whose war-canoe is launched upon majestic rivers and inland seas – He needs no lesser cathedral![42]

People fail to describe God adequately, even with their most descriptive nouns and adjectives because He is a mystery. They all know, feel, and sense that He is 'other-than' them. Gregory wanted people to enter this darkness of unknowing, to wipe their minds free of any anthropomorphisms and to let God make Himself known to them. 'Prayer in this tradition of Christian spirituality is a *via negativa*, a path of "unknowing"; it turns the soul "away from the image" (apophasis), emptying the mind of all efforts to comprehend the holy.'[43]

---

[41] Atwell (ed.), *Gregory of Nyssa,* p. 88.

[42] Fitzgerald, *Indian Spirit,* p. 52.

[43] Atwell (ed.), *Gregory of Nyssa,* p. 88.

To let God make Himself known to humans, one must enter the darkness. The darkness is the unknown.

> Gregory's anthropology was an important contribution to Christian mysticism. Created in God's image, man's soul is like unto God's nature, enabling man intuitively to know God and through purification to become like God.[44]

Luke 17.21 elucidates this reasoning, 'Jesus [said] ... "the kingdom of God is within you"'. Gregory focused on the darker aspects of God, specifically that one cannot see, perceive, or truly know Him. The goal of His spirituality is focused prayer; one is to focus on His total inaccessibility.

If Gregory of Nyssa spoke to the First Nations (of North America) about this Unknown God, they would completely understand. First Nations have always believed that their quests were seeking the Creator and they set out in seclusion, silence, and fasting. In reality, these quests were a response to the call of the Creator. First Nations have always sought this Great Mystery through quests, visions, and dreams.

Native people have a great respect for Creator in their stories even affecting their ways of being. From Francis Laflesche, Omaha, who was the first professional Indigenous anthropologist (1857 - 1932):

> The representation of the medicine man as a nude figure is not a mere fancy ... For in many of the religious rites the priest appeared in such a manner. This nudity is not without its significance, it typifies the utter helplessness of man, when his strength is contrasted with the power of the Great Spirit. With his best intelligence and greatest skill in the use of his hands, man is powerless to bring into existence even so much as the tiniest flower, while out of the force of the will of the Mysterious One, all things in the heaves and earth have come into existence with beauty, grandeur, and majesty.[45]

Every First Nation has a story of the Creator. Indigenous people have a descriptive name, though not a proper name, for Creator,

---

[44] Atwell (ed.), *Gregory of Nyssa*, p. 487.

[45] Fitzgerald, *Indian Spirit*, p. 48.

including these examples: 'Kchi-Manitou',[46] the master spirit (Cree); 'Wakan Tanka',[47] The Great Mystery (Lakota/Sioux); 'The Great Spirit'[48] (Blackfoot, Sac, Pawnee, Shawnee, Mohawk); 'Yudughu', the Being up on high[49] (Carrier); Great Spirit sends 'Kloskurbeh, the Great Teacher'[50] (Abenaki), Hoh-na-when-da-chu[51] (Zuni), He-sa-ke-tv-me-se[52] (Muscogee); and also, 'Wakan Tanka', which is also translated 'The Great Mystery'.[53] Gregory of Nyssa would have appreciated this name for God because he focused on God's transcendence. According to Gregory, 'God is this slippery, steep crag which yields no footholds for our imagination ... What vertigo in the soul this causes!'[54] His method of spirituality is imageless prayer: to meditate on God's incomprehensibility. Gregory said that 'the divine nature ... transcends every act of comprehensive knowledge, and it cannot be approached or attained by one's speculation'.[55]

Although Gregory focused on the transcendence of God, he also had a proficient grasp of the Incarnation. Gregory understood the immanence of the Incarnation, yet he instructed one to seek God *via negativa* and allow God to speak to us – to seek us. The transcendence and immanence of Creator is made clear in Ps. 18.16, 'He reached down from on high and took hold of me and He drew me out of deep waters'.

God is incomprehensible and yet as close as air but finite minds cannot grasp Him. One can witness His attributes and study His characteristics in the Bible, but still cannot fathom His substance or His wisdom or His strength or anything about Him. This is the Creator; this is the Great Mystery, the Great Spirit; this unknowable, unsearchable 'Being up on High'. How can one seek the One

---

[46] Terrence Murphy and Roberto Perin, *A Concise History of Christianity in Canada* (Don Mills: Oxford University Press, 1996), p. 5.

[47] Twiss, *One Church Many Tribes*, p. 94.

[48] Susan Hazen-Hammond, *Through the Centuries with Mother Earth and Father Sky: Timelines of Native American History* (New York: The Berkley Publishing Group, 1997), pp. 192, 109, 104, 98, 92 and 155.

[49] Hall, *The Carrier, My People*, p. 7.

[50] Hall, *The Carrier, My People*, p. 4.

[51] As spoken to the author by a Zuni elder on the Zuni reservation 2006.

[52] As told to the author by a Muscogee elder, 2006.

[53] Nerburn, *The Wisdom of Native Americans*, p. 36.

[54] Cited by Atwell (ed.), *Gregory of Nyssa*, p. 90.

[55] Cited by Atwell (ed.), *Gregory of Nyssa*, p. 89.

who transcends all knowledge? In Jn 6.65 Jesus says, '… no one can come to me unless the Father has enabled him'.

Yet it is very interesting that Gregory studied much and discovered (as far as spirituality) that study was deficient. He would be the perfect Holy Man, Medicine Man, or Shaman for indigenous people. He had a similar method of *seeking* this ominous, unknown Creator and he had the keys for *understanding* this mysterious Creator. Indigenous people can come to know the Unknowable God who is the same Great Mystery revealed through Jesus Christ.

Gregory of Nyssa's style and philosophy are reminiscent of indigenous traditional beliefs. The Creator is not One to be grasped but rather to be sought and served. The western mind must somehow own everything and have complete knowledge in order to explain their faith in a rational way when there is nothing rational about faith. The beauty of Gregory is that he has a great understanding of the Incarnation and this is the next step for indigenous traditional belief, to realize that great love brought Creator to earth.

The Great Mystery of the Incarnation

Sister Archambault (Hunkpapa Lakota) reflects on the gospel as presented to indigenous people. There is neither beauty nor justice in a gospel wrapped in European culture. The moment Christianity becomes real for First Nations is when it is incarnated and accepted into their worldview and not until then. Sister Archambault felt evangelized when she first saw a Native priest in jeans with a long ponytail. She saw Jesus as an indigenous man. Here is more of her insight,

> When we read the Gospel, we must read it as *Native people*, for this is who we are. We can no longer try to be what we think the dominant society wants us to be. As Native Catholic people, we must set out with open minds and hearts; then we will encounter Jesus Christ. We must learn to subtract the chauvinism and the cultural superiority with which this Gospel was often presented to our people. We must, as one author says, 'de-colonize' this Gospel, which said we must become European in order to be Christian. We have to go beyond the *white* gospel in order to perceive its truth.[56]

---

[56] Treat (ed.), *Native and Christian*, p. 135.

The Incarnation of Christ is the single most important aspect of missiology. While Missio Dei tells us mission started in the heart of God, the Incarnation illustrates and exemplifies it. The Incarnation is Missio Dei with skin on.[57] Creator puts skin on and dawns an entirely new day in the mission of God, not to overlook the importance of Missio Dei, but rather to emphasize the reality that Creator came down.

This is the greatest attempt at communication on Creator's behalf in His effort to reach out to humanity. Christ came into a culture and became a learner. If one desires to communicate the gospel of Jesus Christ, that one had better understand the culture of the people to whom they are called. As Lloyd E. Kwast states, '... a thorough understanding of the meaning of culture is prerequisite to any effective communication of God's good news to a different people group'.[58]

Sherwood G. Lingenfelter wrote *Ministering Cross-Culturally: An Incarnational Model for Personal Relationships* while studying the Yapese culture and working on a doctoral dissertation on 'the impact of twenty years of American administration on the Yapese and their culture'.[59] The goal of his book is to make Americans embarking[60] on a cross-cultural ministry aware of some of their individual shortcomings. However, he believes it is not only for missionaries but also for everyone who interacts with people from a different culture. This book proves to be a very useful guide, giving a great deal of insight into cross cultural ministry, and also in assisting one in discovering varying personality traits among missionaries and people in general. It also describes various aspects of the Incarnation, which is relevant to the Theology section of this project.

The Yapese are indigenous Tribal people from the South Pacific and have much in common with indigenous people of Canada and the United States. The differences between Yapese people and

---

[57] A pastor told a story of a small child who was scared to be in his room at night. His mother told him, 'God is here with you', to which the child replied, 'but, I want someone with skin on'.

[58] Lloyd E. Kwast, 'Understanding Culture', in Winter and Hawthorne (eds.), *Perspectives on the World Christian Movement*, p. C-3.

[59] Sherwood G. Lingenfelter and Marvin K. Mayers, *Ministering Cross-Culturally: An Incarnational Model for Personal Relationships* (Grand Rapids: Baker Book House, 2nd edn, 2003), p. 14.

[60] ... and all those with a 'western' mindset.

North Americans are almost exact as indigenous people and therefore Lingenfelter's book is perfect to discover some interesting cultural variations. This book has been useful in providing definitions
and explanations of numerous cultural differences which are also
applicable to the differences between non-indigenous peoples and
indigenous peoples of Canada and the United States.

A First Nations person might not say that culture is the most
important aspect of their life. Yet, as they live their lives, a casual
non-Native observer will notice how immensely culture affects ever
aspect of Native life. 'Culture is the anthropologist's label for the
sum of the distinctive characteristics of a people's way of life. All
human behavior occurs within particular cultures, within socially
defined contexts.'[61]

Lingenfelter's book presents a great method to 'understand interpersonal conflicts between individuals from the same and different cultures'.[62] It is called the Basic Values model, which is a type of
personality test, and is a valuable resource that will help everyone
involved (e.g. the person embarking on a cross-cultural mission and
those who are the recipients). After learning of the Basic Values
model, a Biola University student from the Hispanic culture understood something more of her own cultural identity and no longer
felt isolated because of personal cultural identity differences with
the dominant society. Perhaps potential missionaries should take
this test to determine how successful they would be in cross-
cultural ministry.

The goal of his book is to 'help readers gain a deeper understanding of themselves and the people with whom they live and in
the process to help them experience a deeper relationship with God
and a more fruitful life of love and ministry to others'.[63] Lingenfelter cogently employs his experience with the Yapese culture of
the South Pacific in delineating examples to us of numerous cross-
cultural differences.

---

[61] Lingenfelter and Mayers, *Ministering Cross-Culturally*, p. 17.

[62] Lingenfelter and Mayers, *Ministering Cross-Culturally*, p. 10.

[63] Lingenfelter and Mayers, *Ministering Cross-Culturally*, p. 12.

The Incarnation

God's model for ministry is the Incarnation.[64] Jesus is the 200 percent person. People are 100 percent of the culture in which they live, but since Jesus was fully God and fully human he is 200 percent. There is no way people can incarnate themselves to that degree in a culture other than their own but they can become 150 percent people, endemic to one culture while immersing themselves in another.

The first aspect of the Incarnation is that Jesus came as an infant, helpless and dependent. He did not appear as a fully-grown adult and part of the ruling class. The dependent part is very crucial when dealing with other cultures when interacting with others in a foreign country, many begin to compare the country unfavorably with their own. Jesus did not interface with those in other cultures by approaching them as a ruler or someone who superior to them. The people of any nation or culture will be repulsed by outsiders whose approach is heavy-handed. Even teachers who are entering a country to present a theology course should first submit themselves to the culture and allow themselves to be learners – ask any leader in Mexico if this is appropriate and their answer will be a surprise. People can personally and spiritually benefit so much if they are humble and enter unfamiliar situations with a willingness to learn from others.

Jesus was not born with special knowledge; He learned and matured as did every member of his society. He learned carpentry, the Scriptures and worship from his elders. 'In Luke 2:46, we read that Mary and Joseph found Jesus in the temple, listening to the teachers of the law and asking them questions. This is a profound statement: The Son of God was sitting in the temple, listening and questioning!'[65] Jesus was not simply 100 percent human, he was 100 percent Jewish. Jesus was immersed in the Jewish culture and drew from those experiences on a daily basis to bring to life the Gospels as they are known today. 'Culture, then, is the conceptual design, the definitions by which people order their lives, interpret their experiences, and evaluate the behavior of others.'[66] By being learners of

---

[64] Lingenfelter and Mayers, *Ministering Cross-Culturally*, p. 13.

[65] Lingenfelter and Mayers, *Ministering Cross-Culturally*, p. 16.

[66] Lingenfelter and Mayers, *Ministering Cross-Culturally*, p. 18.

the culture to which one is called, one can avoid 'misunderstanding, confusion, and oftentimes interpersonal conflict'.[67] Every culture gives cues. For example, Lingenfelter tells the story of initiating and terminating a conversation. In the United States it is usually the suggestion of a cup of coffee and the people terminate the conversation by excusing themselves or saying it's time to go. However in the Yapese culture they will offer one a betel nut to chew to initiate the conversation and then say, 'It is time for you to leave', when the conversation is over. This may be considered rude in our culture but to them it is quite normal. Without this knowledge a missionary could feel very hurt or offended at the end of a conversation. However, a missionary could also insult a Yapese person if they misunderstood the invitation to chew a betel nut, thinking they were merely being offered a snack to share instead of an entire conversation.

Lingenfelter insists that the goal of incarnation be kept in view because each person is part of a social context and culture and it is from that context that one reacts to every situation. However, as has been noted in the above example, sometimes one's culture can lead an individual in the opposite or at least a mistaken direction. People are acculturated in their own context. Incarnational ministry requires a great deal of humility. It is not for the proud or for the stubborn; it is for those who desperately want to see Jesus transform lives in another culture.

Lingenfelter shows that there are many differences between the Yapese people and himself as an American. The Yapese people have a very different concept of time than Americans. This also applies to Native people who have different concepts of time from Americans and Canadians. In certain examples Lingenfelter reveals that there was embarrassment and shame caused by a White missionary among the Yapese because she was upset that a meeting was going on too long. She impatiently rang the bell which ended the service; the visiting pastor was embarrassed and closed his sermon, and the local pastor was embarrassed. After apologizing to the visiting pastor, he later told the missionary that they did not mind going well overtime because they were happy to have their

---

[67] Lingenfelter and Mayers, *Ministering Cross-Culturally*, p. 18.

visitor. It seems that this conflict relating to differing concepts of time embarrassed everyone.

According to Lingenfelter's chart,[68] an American or Canadian will forgive one for arriving five minutes late, a Latin American will forgive one for being thirty minutes late and a Yapese will forgive two hours of lateness. However, an American or Canadian will feel hostility and anger if one is more than thirty minutes late. This span is much longer for Latin Americans (two hours) while the Yapese will not be happy if one is over four hours late.

The Yapese and Latin American are closer to the Native people of the United States and Canada than to the American/Canadian view of time. A meeting is to begin when everyone is present as opposed to a scheduled time. The relationships are more important than being on time and waiting is not a problem because the idea of gathering for an event is the most important component, some-times even more so than the event itself.

Another glaring difference between Lingenfelter's American cul-ture and the Yapese culture is crisis/non-crisis orientations. He gives an example of an impending hurricane announcement on the radio which did not produce a response from the Yapese locals. They deal with things as they come whereas Americans plan and even train (military) for an impending crisis. Lingenfelter warns against a person from a crisis oriented culture becoming overly judgmental in these situations. He also states that there are people within each culture who defy these cultural boxes into which others try to place them. There are also Americans who are chronically late and Yapese who prepare for disasters. However, since these are not in the majority, it is realistic to make these generalizations.

Another difference involves tasks. Certain people are very task-oriented while others are person-oriented. They can clash if they work on the same team because each utilizes a different method in conducting their lives. Task-oriented people will often overlook people in order to complete a project they have started. Person-oriented people are more likely to overlook details, projects, dead-lines, and reports, and instead prioritize relationships. Similar per-sonality traits can also be found in both Americans and Yapese, however, there are overarching societal contexts which suggest

---

[68] Lingenfelter and Mayers, *Ministering Cross-Culturally*, p. 39.

Americans are more task-oriented while Yapese are more people-oriented.

> American society views negatively the highly social but nonproductive person, while Micronesian societies disapprove of the individual who appears to be hard, unkind, and striving. For mission work, these differences suggest that the most productive Americans may not be the best people to send to interaction-oriented non-western cultures and that the most productive nationals may not be the best candidates for church leadership ... We need to reassess the standards by which we select missionaries and nationals to be church leaders and by which we recognize them for service.[69]

This is a key point for the improvement of Native and non-Native relations. Native people are people-oriented and live in a dominant society that values increasing productivity. He warns the task-oriented people, 'This means the task-oriented individual must consciously allocate significant amounts of time to sit and talk with people, for without a conscious effort, tasks will exhaust all available time and energy'.[70] Lingenfelter then discusses the biblical mandate emphasizing the importance of people over goals or tasks. No task is of greater value than people.[71] Jesus exemplifies this when He does not grieve, eat, or pray, but rather continues to minister to people out of his compassion (Lk. 9.9).

The main Scripture Lingenfelter references throughout the book is 1 Cor. 9.22, 23. 'I have become all things to all men so that by all possible means I might save some. I do all this for the sake of the gospel that I may share in its blessings.'

He insists that 'the goal of becoming partially incarnate in the culture of those to whom we minister is, by God's grace, within our grasp'.[72] Having an Incarnational ministry also means accepting the 'host culture as a valid, albeit imperfect, way of life'.[73] The term 'imperfect' is used because not every culture reflects Biblical values; many have immoral or unethical attitudes and behaviors. However,

---

[69] Lingenfelter and Mayers, *Ministering Cross-Culturally*, pp. 81, 82.

[70] Lingenfelter and Mayers, *Ministering Cross-Culturally*, p. 84.

[71] Lingenfelter and Mayers, *Ministering Cross-Culturally*, p. 86.

[72] Lingenfelter and Mayers, *Ministering Cross-Culturally*, p. 119.

[73] Lingenfelter and Mayers, *Ministering Cross-Culturally*, p. 119.

he is careful to point out that each culture has a story, a history that has led them to where they are now which serves to give them their uniqueness. That is an important aspect of becoming Incarnational; hear the stories. Lingenfelter persistently asserts that one must 'learn about and participate in their culture'.[74] He concludes with this, 'The goal of this book has been to show that the incarnation of Christ is a powerful analogy for missionary and other Christian ministry'.

This book is a wonderful guide to Incarnational ministry and the principles should be read by anyone called to ministry among the indigenous people of Canada and the United States. It is the author's opinion that, unfortunately these principles are almost never applied to indigenous ministry within Canada and the United States. There are bright spots dotting the continent but instead of incarnational ministry, indigenous people are usually requested to give up something personal or nonessential in order to come to Christ.

Theology of the Land

Native people believe that Creator placed them on their land and gave it to them, not to own in the British common-law property ownership sense – but rather to care for it. Indigenous people see the Earth as special and alive. They also believe that one is connected to it and call it Mother Earth. This is a very wholesome and Biblical view of the Earth. Unfortunately not all people have a positive view of the earth, even Christians.

> Some Christians, we must admit, hold a view of Christian faith that does not have much place in it for earth-keeping. But is this true of the biblical story that allegedly informs the Christian worldview? Far from it![75]

Those Christians not interested in earth-keeping are products of years of anthropological (e.g. man centered) theology that overlooks Creation. Unless they have been acculturated, Native people have never believed or agreed with the viewpoint of these Christians. In

---

[74] Lingenfelter and Mayers, *Ministering Cross-Culturally*, p. 120.

[75] Iain Provan, The Land is Mine and You Are Only Tenants (Leviticus 25:23): Earth-keeping and People-keeping in the Old Testament, *CRUX* 42.2 (Summer 2006), p. 3.

1967, Lynn White Jr.[76] wrote an article, *The Historical Roots of Our Ecological Crisis,* describing the devastation of the environment due to the worldview of Christianity. White calls Christianity anthropocentric because of *imago dei* and the mandate in Genesis that man has dominion over the earth and animals, which have no soul. Many Christians have refuted White and shown that the Bible truly does talk about earth-keeping. However, most Christians have not held a constructive view of creation and have been anthropocentric. There is hope because the Bible does uphold the importance of land to which Native people can relate.

> … Native Christians have an opportunity to receive the Bible and to be shaped by it without falling into the traps of modern western culture. To state this another way, when thinking about Aboriginal perspectives on land, go to Scripture directly. Do not go through the lens of modern perspectives on land and spirituality. Modern western Christians have contextualized the Bible in their cultural context. Aboriginal Christians need not accept that. But we believe that they can find congenial dialogue partners on the margins of western cultural Christianity.[77]

Stan McKay, Fisher River Cree, a former moderator in the United Church of Canada (1992), states that there are parallels between the identity of Natives and identity of biblical Israelites. They are founded in a relationship between humanity, creation, and Creator.[78] He encourages Christians to think of Native people as 'Old Testament people' because of the vast similarities such as 'oral tradition which is rooted in the Creator and the creation. Like Moses, one knows about the sacredness of the earth and the promise of land. Creation stories also emphasize the power of the Creator and the goodness of creation.'[79]

Materialism poses the greatest threat against creation. The wealth of developed countries continues to grow while the majority

---

[76] Lynn Townsend White, Jr., 'The Historical Roots of Our Ecologic Crisis', *Science* 155.3767 (March 10, 1967), pp. 1203-207.

[77] Jonathan Dyck and Cornelius Buller, 'Mapping the Land: Toward an Aboriginal Biblical Theology of Land', *Journal of North American Institute for Indigenous Theological Studies* 2.2 (2004), p. 68.

[78] Treat (ed.), *Native and Christian*, p. 51.

[79] Treat (ed.), *Native and Christian*, p. 52.

of the world suffers harsh poverty; and yet, First Nations people greatly desire to work together with non-Native people to see health restored to their corner of the planet.

Missiology

Paul the Apostle as Missionary

The Apostle Paul epitomizes contextualization to the Gentiles as a palpable model for modern Christians. With his feet firmly planted in his roots of Judaism, the Apostle contextualized the Good News of Jesus Christ to the Gentiles (and specifically to the Greeks). Christians today should copy his commitment to Christ and to contextualization in order to witness others come to Christ. Contextualization is ministry performed in the context of the people themselves.

Paul has proven to be one of the strongest voices in the New Testament for advancing sound missiology. This section of this project contains an overview of Paul's missiological principles. Paul's approach to the Greek culture will be considered with regard to evangelism towards First Nations. By a simple, cursory reading the Acts of the Apostles,[80] Paul's method is easily recognized through his message and his actions. Later in this section, the manner in which the Apostle Paul's methods affect ministry to First Nations will be discussed.

At Paul's conversion, God calls him to preach the Good News to the Gentiles and to suffer: '... This man is my chosen instrument to carry my name before the Gentiles and their kings and before the people of Israel. I will show him how much he must suffer for my name' (Acts 9.15, 16). In this passage, God names the Gentiles first. Later in Acts 13.47, one hears Paul reiterate his call (and he includes Barnabas), 'For this is what the Lord commanded us: I have made you a light for the Gentiles, that you may bring salvation to the ends of the earth'. Paul refers to himself as 'the apostle to the Gentiles (Rom. 1.5; 11.13; 15.16; Gal. 2.7-10; Eph. 3.5-8)'.[81] Michael Barram in his book, *Mission and Moral Reflection in Paul,* tells us 'Paul understands himself to be entrusted with a mission. He refers often

---

[80] All Scriptures in this missiological section are quoted from the Acts of the Apostles unless otherwise noted.

[81] Wright, *What Saint Paul Really Said*, p. 78.

to his apostolic calling to the Gentiles' (footnoting Rom. 1.1, 5; 1 Cor. 1.1; 2 Cor. 1.1; Gal. 1.1; 2.8; see also Rom. 11.13; 1 Cor. 4.9; 9.1, 2; 15.9; Gal. 1.17; 1 Thess. 2.7; cf. 1 Cor. 11.5; 12.11, 12).[82]

A few scholars claim that this mission is of crucial importance for an adequate grasp of Paul's letters and thought. (See Baird, *Paul's Message and Mission* etc.) Indeed, some – missiologists, in particular – who consider mission to be of seminal concern, have even suggested the need for a 'missiological hermeneutic', an interpretive strategy directed toward the equipping of present-day Christian communities for their life and witness in the world.[83]

A cursory reading of Acts will include this missiological hermeneutic providing clues to Paul's method of evangelism.

Paul's preparation for mission to the Gentiles was unique. Although immersed in his native Hebrew teachings, and raised to be a Pharisee, he was born in Tarsus where he would have learned the Greek culture and language. In Acts, Paul is seen as a master of articulation and a perfect fit for missions to Gentiles because of the contemporary Greek philosophy. Paul used convincing oratory common for his day especially in Athens, which was the perfect place to philosophize new ideas and to facilitate Paul's preaching of the gospel to the Gentiles (Acts 17.21). Greek philosophy is also commonly accepted today by people with a 'western' frame of mind except for the indigenous people who have an altogether different perspective. Arguing and reasoning is not always the best approach to evangelize Native people.

For the last ten years or more, a new word has been used to describe the current 'western' state of mind: postmodern. The basic thinking behind postmodernity is a great disillusionment with modernism, which cherishes the meta-story and deals in absolutes, especially regarding science and religion. Postmodernism rejects formulas, fixed ideas; and therefore absolute truth becomes questionable.

---

[82] Darrell L. Guder (ed.), *Missional Church: A Vision for the Sending of the Church in North America* (Grand Rapids: Eerdmans, 1998), p. 4. See also Michael Barram, *Mission and Moral Reflection in Paul* (New York: Peter Lang, 2006).

[83] Guder (ed.), *Missional Church*, p. 4; Barram, *Mission and Moral Reflection in Paul*, p. 11.

Postmodern accurately describes the mindset of an indigenous person. Therefore, when the postmodern philosophy recently arrived, most First Nations wryly thought, 'It's about time'. When it comes to religion, most Traditional[84] Native people will always wonder how, and more so, *why* the White Man will reduce the Great Mystery[85] to a few systematic declarations.

The Apostle Paul's philosophy was far from the reducing of God to a few morals, laws, or creeds. While he knew about them and their importance, he also walked in the Holy Spirit. To him the role of the Spirit was central:

> Through the death and resurrection of his Son Jesus, our Lord, a gracious and loving God has effected eschatological salvation for his new covenant people, the church, who now, as they await Christ's coming, live the life of the future by the power of the Spirit ... Any understanding of Paul that does not recognize the crucial role of the Spirit in his theology quite misses Paul's own concerns and emphases.[86]

The emphasis on the Holy Spirit is not only evident in Paul's writings but also in the Acts of the Apostles where the Holy Spirit is manifest throughout. Even when Paul is confronting a sorcerer, he is fearless, because as is stated in Acts 13.9, 'Paul, filled with the Holy Spirit ...' looks straight at the man, sets him straight and leaves him temporarily blind so that another person can believe in Jesus, and not be blinded by the sorcerer's lies.

With the Holy Spirit as his guide, years of experience in learning the Torah, having been raised in the midst of a Greek culture, living under Roman rule while maintaining his Jewish identity, Paul was a missiologist waiting to happen. Perhaps God chose Paul because of his fierce dedication to his faith; however, it required the Holy Spirit to remove the scales from his eyes for him to realize the Truth of Jesus as Messiah in Acts 9.17, 18.

---

[84] The term 'Traditional' describes a First Nations person who follows the original traditions, ways, and beliefs of their people.

[85] The Great Mystery is one of the descriptions of God found among the Native people. The Theology section of this project will expand on these views of God.

[86] Gordon Fee, *God's Empowering Presence* (Peabody, MA: Hendrickson, 2002), p. 13.

Then Ananias went to the house and entered it. Placing his hands on Saul, he said, 'Brother Saul, the Lord – Jesus, who appeared to you on the road as you were coming here – has sent me so that you may see again and be filled with the Holy Spirit. Immediately, something like scales fell from Saul's eyes, and he could see again. He got up and was baptized.

It is the Holy Spirit who gives one power to witness as Jesus said in Acts 1.8, 'But you will receive power when the Holy Spirit comes on you; and you will be my witnesses in Jerusalem, and in all Judea and Samaria, and to the ends of the earth'. Paul relied upon the Holy Spirit to preach the Good News. It is also the key to being an effective evangelist.

Paul's Christian brothers did not easily accept him. They remembered him as a great threat to their lives and wondered if his conversion was a ruse to locate and uncover them. Even though he had an encounter with Jesus himself, and was filled with the Spirit, it took another Christian named Barnabas to introduce Paul to the others.

Paul has no need for assimilation: be ye circumcised

In Acts 10, Peter has a dream that would change the appearance of Christianity. In his dream, followed by the immediate circumstances, God reveals to him that Gentiles believe and are filled with the Holy Spirit. His friends and fellow Christian Judaizers struggle with these concepts and initially reprimand Peter for going to a house of 'uncircumcised men' (11.3) and eating with them. Peter tells them that God filled them with the Holy Spirit and who was he to oppose God? 'When they heard this, they had no further objections and praised God, saying, "So then, God has granted even the Gentiles repentance unto life"' (11.18).

These events are a prelude to the Jerusalem Council in Acts 15. If God had not spoken to Peter that the Gentiles could be saved through grace, perhaps circumcision would still be a significant part of becoming a Christian today.

Paul and Barnabas were ministering among the Gentiles in Antioch. They received some brothers from Judea who began preaching salvation through circumcision. The Judean brothers taught, '... Unless you are circumcised, according to the custom taught by Moses, you cannot be saved' (15.1). Paul and Barnabas sharply disagreed with these men. They went as a delegation that would bring this disagreement to Jerusalem to the apostles and elders. In Jerusalem, believers who were Pharisees argued that all must obey the Law of Moses. They discussed the subject extensively until Peter stood and reminded them how the Lord had spoken to him about the Gentiles:

> ... Brothers, you know that some time ago God made a choice among you that the Gentiles might hear from my lips the message of the gospel and believe. God, who knows the heart, showed that he accepted them by giving the Holy Spirit to them, just as he did to us. He made no distinction between us and them, for he purified their hearts by faith. Now then, why do you try to test God by putting on the necks of the disciples a yoke that neither we nor our fathers have been able to bear? No! We believe it is through the grace of our Lord Jesus that we are saved, just as they are (Acts 15.7-11).

They then heard testimony from Paul and Barnabas about the miraculous signs and wonders God was doing among the Gentiles and later James brought evidence from the Torah that the Gentiles are welcome to seek the Lord. They all agreed that circumcision was too difficult and an unnecessary barrier for Gentile Christians and wrote a letter explaining their rationale. The result of the Jerusalem Council regarding the Gentiles adapting Jewish religious culture is,

> It seemed good to the Holy Spirit and to us not to burden you with anything beyond the following requirements: You are to abstain from food sacrificed to idols, from blood, from the meat of strangled animals and from sexual immorality. You will do well to avoid these things (Acts 15.28-29).

Peter, Paul, and Barnabas won a great victory for the Gentile believers that day. The Gentile believers did not need circumcision, which was a Jewish custom, as a requirement for salvation. This is contextualization of the gospel for the Gentile believers. Paul does not 'shout his message across a yawning cultural gap'.[87] He becomes all things to all people as it says in 1 Cor. 9.22, '... so that by all

---

[87] Wright, *What Saint Paul Really Said*, p. 80.

possible means I might save some'. Paul was able to speak to the Jews about being a Jew but also understood that other cultures should not be subject to Jewish religious laws.

Paul becomes all things to all people: contextualizes himself
In Acts 16, Paul circumcises a Gentile (Timothy). Why would Paul debate against circumcision in Acts 15 and then circumcise Timothy in chapter 16? It seems bizarre to those unfamiliar with Jewish culture.

Missiologically, Acts 16 is miles away from chapter 15. Chapter 15 overrules the Judaizers' insurmountable requirements for Gentiles who become Christian. Gentiles did not have to accept Jewish religious ways, culture, and customs in order to accept Jesus, while chapter 16 involves ministry to Jews. In chapter 16, Paul circumcises Timothy before a missionary journey, '... because of the Jews who lived in that area, for they all knew that his father was a Greek' (16.3). In this passage, Paul helps Timothy *become all things to all people*. If this passage is not read missiologically, it does not make much sense.

In Acts 11 Peter explains his visit with Cornelius, a Gentile, to the Jewish believers. The Jewish believers rightly corrected Peter based on their religious views stating that Peter entered a house of uncircumcised men and shared a meal: these actions were inappropriate for a Jew. (However, because of the Holy Spirit, Peter was able to persuade the Judaizers that God was responsible for his visit and he was not being disobedient). Based on their religious beliefs, the Jews were right to question Peter's actions. Therefore, if Paul wanted to minister to Jewish people, they would have every right to question why he was associating with Timothy, an uncircumcised man, and the ministry *would not happen*. Here we see Paul contextualizing Timothy at a painful cost in order to facilitate ministry.

This precedent applies to First Nations ministry. Anyone who desires to perform ministry among First Nations people must contextualize himself or herself. It is not as palpable as circumcision, but perhaps it can be just as painful.

Paul uses objects and words from another culture to preach Good News
Acts 17 finds Paul in Athens waiting for Silas and Timothy. While walking around the city Paul '... was greatly distressed to see that the city was full of idols' (17.16). In Acts 17.22, Paul stands up and

speaks. The first thing he does is acknowledge that the Athenians are very religious. He does not begin by shaming them or being condescending but rather Paul opens a door of discussion. He begins with a compliment on their spirituality.

The next topic Paul chooses is directly from the Athenian culture, '... An Unknown God ...' (17.23). He employed something from their culture to bring about the Truth. Paul rejects the 'Unknown God' and reveals the True God, who is not contained in stone or wood. In fact, Paul takes on their idols without demeaning their gods but rather by explaining God's true nature. He begins by giving God a description: Creator. How, in the form of a temple, can humans capture in a temple the One who made everything? How can humans equip the Creator who consistently supplies them life and breath, and everything?

Then Paul does something truly beautiful. In Acts 17.28 he quotes their sacred writings, '"For in him we live and move and have our being." As some of your own poets have said, "We are his offspring".' The *NIV Study Bible* offers further insight,

> [Acts] 17:28 *some of your own poets.* There are two quotations here: (1) 'In him we live and move and have our being,' from the Cretan poet Epimenides (c. 600 B.C.) in his *Cretica*, and (2) 'We are his offspring,' from the Cilician poet Aratus (c. 315-240) in his *Phaenomena*, as well as from Cleanthes (331-233) in his *Hymn to Zeus*. Paul quotes Greek poets elsewhere as well (see 1 Cor. 15:33; Titus 1:12 and notes).

How often does one hear modern missionaries quoting ancient sources of the people to whom they are ministering? There is spirituality in every nation of the world and a view of God from which every missionary can begin teaching.

Paul does not blaspheme
In Acts 19, we find Paul getting into some trouble in Ephesus. Signs and wonders follow Paul's ministry and we even see people healed by cloths that had touched Paul.

Then a silversmith named Demetrius (19.23) begins a riot against Paul. A great and angry crowd rushed Paul's companions into the theater where 'the whole city was in an uproar' (19.29). The main complaint Demetrius had was that his idol making business would be ruined and their god Artemis would not be worshipped. He says that Paul,

> ... convinced and led astray large numbers of people here in Ephesus and in practically the whole province of Asia. (Paul) says that man-made gods are no gods at all. There is danger not only that our trade will lose its good name, but also that that temple of the great goddess Artemis will be discredited, and the goddess herself, who is worshipped throughout the province of Asia and the world, will be robbed of her divine majesty (Acts 19.26-27).

The demonstration was so dangerous that even province officials sent Paul a message not to stand before the riotous crowd. After two hours of shouting the city clerk was able to speak to the crowd. The main defense for Paul and his friends was, '... they have neither robbed temples nor blasphemed our goddess' (19.37). The city clerk stated that the riot was for nothing and dismissed the crowd.

It is astonishing that Paul escaped and did not blaspheme Artemis.[88] In all of his preaching and teaching, Paul did not blaspheme the goddess of the Ephesians. He only spoke the truth about God and prayed for healing and deliverance for the people. The riot took place because many people had come to faith, not because Paul felt the need to denigrate their goddess in order to exalt Jesus.

Paul continues Jewish purification ceremonies
In Acts 21, Paul arrives in Jerusalem. He tells James and all the elders the great news of the ministry among the Gentiles and they praise God, before informing Paul that,

> ... thousands of Jews have believed, and all of them are zealous for the law. They have been informed that you teach all the Jews who live among the Gentiles to turn away from Moses, telling them not to circumcise their children or live according to our customs. What shall we do? (Acts 21.20-22)

They immediately make plans to prove to the Jews that Paul is '... living in obedience to the law' (21.24). '[Paul] purified himself

---

[88] Pastor Jack W. Hayford noted this during a School of Pastoral Nurture, January 2006.

along with them. Then he went to the temple to give notice of the date when the days of purification would end and the offering would be made for each of them' (21.26).

However, Paul also discusses how believers are justified by Christ, *not by following the law*. In Gal. 2.1-14, Paul reprimands Peter for disassociating with Gentile believers in Antioch because of the other Jews. Peter is 'afraid of those who belonged to the circumcision group' (Gal. 2.12). In confronting Peter, Paul spells out exactly what circumcision and the law means,

> When I saw that they were not acting in line with the truth of the gospel, I said to Peter in front of them all, 'You are a Jew, yet you live like a Gentile and not like a Jew. How is it, then, that you force Gentiles to follow Jewish customs?' We who are Jews by birth and not Gentile sinners know that a man is not justified by observing the law, but by faith in Jesus Christ. So we, too, have put our faith in Christ Jesus that we may be justified by faith in Christ and not by observing the law, because by observing the law no one will be justified. If, while we seek to be justified in Christ, it becomes evident that we ourselves are sinners, does that mean that Christ promotes sin? Absolutely not! If I rebuild what I destroyed, I prove that I am a lawbreaker. For through the law I died to the law so that I might live for God. I have been crucified with Christ and I no longer live, but Christ lives in me. The life I live in the body, I live by faith in the Son of God, who loved me and gave himself for me. I do not set aside the grace of God, for if righteousness could be gained through the law, Christ died for nothing (Gal. 2.14-21).

How is one to interpret these two Scriptures? Does Paul contradict himself? No, he does not. If one views Paul's partaking in purification ceremonies through a missiological hermeneutic, one can perfectly understand him.

In Acts, Paul was making a statement to the Jewish believers. He was showing the Jews that he himself was a Jew. He contextualized himself in order to be able to preach the gospel to his own people.

Paul speaks in their heart language
Soon after this, Paul is defending himself against the Jews in Jerusalem. He is speaking to a Roman commander in Greek but then changes languages to address the crowd in Aramaic. 'When they

heard him speak to them in Aramaic, they became very quiet'
(22.2). There is something special about speaking to people in their
language. They are able to understand.

Paul begins by explaining who he is and then relates the Damascus road experience when he met Jesus. When he talks about Ananias, notice that he does it in a Jewish context, 'A man named Ananias came to see me. He was a devout observer of the law and highly respected by all the Jews living there' (22.12). In Acts 9, all one reads about Ananias is that he is a disciple (9.10). Paul is telling the crowd the truth but he is emphasizing aspects that will assuage the angry Jewish crowd.

In Acts 9.17, Ananias names Jesus to Paul:

> Then Ananias went to the house and entered it. Placing his hands on Saul, he said, 'Brother Saul, the Lord – Jesus, who appeared to you on the road as you were coming here – has sent me so that you may see again and be filled with the Holy Spirit.'

Later, in Acts 22.14, Paul uses different words to convey this message to the Jewish audience. He inserts the phrase 'the God of our fathers' and repeats the conversation with Ananias using a different term for Jesus,

> Then [Ananias] said: 'The God of our fathers has chosen you to know his will and to see the Righteous One and to hear words from his mouth. You will be his witness to all men of what you have seen and heard. And now what are you waiting for? Get up, be baptized and wash your sins away, calling on his name' (Acts 22.14-16).

The point of this study of Acts is not to present an exhaustive study of the names or words of the New and Old Testament and their usage. Nor is the point to test oral tradition or Paul's ability to recount Ananias' every word. The focus of this study is to illustrate that every good communicator will contextualize his or her message for the audience to which they are speaking. It simply requires good communication skills. One can appreciate in the last several examples, Paul is a master communicator. He can shift between Greek and Aramaic. He can stand in front of a crowd and tell them the truth, without making them angry and unable to receive his message. Paul's words made his Jewish audience sit up and listen because he is speaking their heart language, using familiar phraseology. This is not to suggest that one deny Jesus – Paul did not deny Jesus in these verses. He simply chose the most appropriate words to be relevant to the audience recognizing that the crowd was 'trying to kill him' (21.31).

Paul lets them know who he is
In Acts 22, Paul informs the Roman commander that he was born a Roman citizen. The commander is '... alarmed when he realized that he had put Paul, a Roman citizen, in chains' (Acts 22.29). This circumstance gives Paul the right to be tried in a Roman court.

The next day when Paul stands before the Sanhedrin, he tells them, 'My brothers, I am a Pharisee, the son of a Pharisee' (Acts 23.6). Paul uses every means possible and takes every opportunity to ensure that the gospel is preached.

> You know that I have not hesitated to preach anything that would be helpful to you but have taught you publicly and from house to house. I have declared to both Jews and Greeks that they must turn to God in repentance and have faith in our Lord Jesus (Acts 20.20-21).

What does the Apostle Paul teach us about indigenous ministry in Canada and the United States? Can Paul, the Apostle in Acts, teach one how to do First Nations ministry? The Acts of the Apostles offers clues about how he related to people and situations and depicts how Paul utilized proper missiological concepts. In the following section, Paul's methods, as they relate to First Nations ministry, will be reviewed. In one small book of the Bible, considerable useful information may be gleaned to assist one when talking about the Way.

First Nations

First Nations – no need for assimilation: be ye circumcised.
In Acts 15, the disciples in Jerusalem discuss whether Gentiles should be subject to Jewish religious rites and traditions. After much discussion (Paul gave testimony but even more important is Peter's testimony about Cornelius in Acts 11), they decide not to burden the Gentiles with the perquisite to be circumcised (15.7-11). They do cite several requirements but not as many as they as Jews must follow. This is an interesting discussion for every church or

ministry. When one engages the mission field, or those who have newly come to faith, one should not rush to impose a list of rules and regulations.

Some people will not attend church for fear of an overwhelming 'list of do's and don'ts'. They are talking about the threshold for entering a church, which can be set very high. There are examples in stories of a hippie, or a biker, or a homeless person who entered a church and no one knew what to do because this person did not fit in with how a 'church person' should look.

One night at the author's son's Youth Group, Pastor Steve Hibdon from Florence Ave. Foursquare Church dressed like a homeless person, complete with a shopping cart, and sat outside the entrance of the youth building. No one recognized him so he was able to hear the youth's first impression. Some of the kids said 'Hi', others said, 'Go away!', but only one young man talked to him and even gave him a Bible. Later, Pastor Steve highly commended this young man for reaching out to him. However, the Youth Group has well over sixty youth attending! Pastor Steve taught the teens a great lesson that night – do not overlook someone because of differences – talk to them about The Way.

First Nations people are continually subjected to circumcision, not of the flesh, but of their culture. First Nation songs, dances, regalia, instruments, and song style are beautiful and should be encouraged in church. In fact these cultural aspects *must* be a part of any indigenous Church in order to be authentic before God.

First Nations – becoming all things to all people: contextualize one's self
Paul circumcised Timothy before he began ministering to Jews who would have rejected, not the message of the gospel, but the messenger, because Jewish law forbids them to associate with the uncircumcised. As previously stated in Acts 11.3 the Jews properly criticized Peter for associating with Gentiles (those uncircumcised).

How does this relate to First Nations people? This section is subtitled 'contextualize one's self'. When one visits a First Nations Reservation, village, or church, will they change appearance or learn a new culture?

For Native people a non-Native can grow out their hair into a pony-tail (for a man), learn to speak the Native language, learn proper protocol, learn to be quiet and not do all the talking and never, never wear a suit and tie unless they are going to a funeral, and even then they may be overdressed. However, each of these above items will not ensure success. Some Reservations own casinos and the people there dress better than those in Hollywood, so if one wants to minister there, they might want to dress up a little. Not every Native group traditionally had long hair in a ponytail, but more and more this has become a symbol of their identity.

Those desiring to be involved on a Reserve or in First Nations Urban ministry must change certain ways or habits; otherwise they will utterly fail because their culture sometimes speaks louder than their intended message. In Paul's case, the Jews would not even listen to him if Timothy remained uncircumcised.

A Korean mission team went into a village in their van and began picking up children and taking them to a neighboring village (only about ten kilometers away) to give them haircuts. They did not first ask the parent's permission. They had a professional hairdresser who was willing to give free haircuts and they also provided a Vacation Bible School on that particular Reserve.

Does this sound like a good way to do missions? To most people a free haircut sounds great. However, to Native people who had their children forcibly taken out of their homes by the government and the church (working together in the Indian Boarding Schools). This was a horrendous idea. What the Koreans did not know was that when the children were taken to Boarding Schools their heads were shaved (boys) or cut (girls) to a 'proper' short haircut. They also did not know that the goal of the Boarding Schools was assimilation which left a deep wound on the indigenous people all across Canada and the United States.

Three hundred miles away, the author received a call about this team. Everyone on the Reserve was angry and demanded to know who these people were, why they were taking the children to another Reserve, who thought they needed haircuts, and could they have asked first?

The Koreans were innocent in the eyes of their own culture. A haircut is good, helping children is good, taking kids ten kilometers is not too far, and the Vacation Bible School was a means to preach the gospel.

Every single indigenous person on that Reserve knew the history of the Indian Boarding Schools and the deep scar they left on their people. The Koreans did not know the history or they did not make the connection. They broke the trust of those dear First Nations people because they did not know any better.

Throw away any thought that one knows what is best for Indian people. Throw away any pity one may feel for them because one cannot befriend someone they consider pitiful. Do not enter a Reservation without permission from the Chief. Alternatively, support others who have an invitation.

Contextualizing yourself means that one becomes a learner. Walk into every situation humbly. One might believe that asking questions is a good way to learn. Perhaps that is true in American or Canadian culture but it is not true among Native people. People learn by observing and doing. If someone keeps asking questions, Native people will get annoyed. This is one of the main differences between indigenous people and White culture, *High and Low culture.* (High and Low culture are explained in the Theology – Anthropology section.)

First Nations – use objects and words from one's culture to preach Good News.
There are many books with quotes from great Chiefs. Many Elders can tell stories of Great Chiefs. If one carefully studies a culture, one will find redemptive aspects. Paul, distressed by the many idols in Athens, begins speaking to the people from their point of view. He begins by talking about something in their culture, using it to tell the truth about Creator. He also quotes their poets, pointing out truths about God. He is speaking their heart language. They can easily understand him. If he began his talk by stating, 'These are false gods and idols', no one would have likely listened to him. However, he identifies with them on familiar ground so they are all able to journey together.

All indigenous people are on a journey to Creator because there are few, if any, Native atheists. People must do their best to journey alongside of them, not in front of them or pushing behind, but alongside.

First Nations – do not blaspheme
The first thing the author heard in Bible School about her people is that Indians follow idols and false gods. In a class on World Religions, the teacher placed numerous pictures on an overhead. Buddha, Krishna, and various symbols appeared, and the teacher explained the significance of each. Then an overhead appeared that

was cause for great alarm: it was a Totem Pole. Immediate discussion on this presentation resulted in the repudiation of the teacher's claims that this was an idol and explained that Native people use Totem Poles to tell a story of a family or a great Chief and sometimes they direct one to a good fishing spot. However, the Totem Pole should not be in the teacher's list of false gods. Another source claimed that Totem Poles *are a conduit for evil spirits*. This person obviously never asked a Native person a question about the Totems. These claims have no bearing in truth. Christians should not make allegations without any proof or knowledge of reality.

Native people have always believed in Creator. No matter where one goes on a Reservation in the United States or a Reserve in Canada, there will be a descriptive name for Creator. If Paul did not believe it was necessary to blaspheme Artemis, one should not do it today. One should follow the Apostle Paul's example and tell the truth about Creator. Choose a less judgmental path of evangelism. No true Christian appreciates making overbearing or insulting remarks regarding atheists so why not act differently? As former Foursquare President Paul Risser said, help people see the church as redemptive and not judgmental.

First Nations – continue to use Ceremonies
Comparing the accounts in Acts and in Gal 2.11-21 is not a problem for the author as a First Nations follower of the Way. There is no contradiction in the author's thinking that Paul can perform a purification ceremony while believing that Christ performed the final work of cleansing and purification on the cross.

Native people have a ceremony called the Smudge. This is a cleansing or purification ceremony that cleanses body, soul, and spirit. Lighting sage, sweet grass, or cedar and then blowing out the fire causes it to smoke in a large abalone shell. The person who desires cleansing pulls the smoke onto themselves and *washes* with it. The smell of the sage, sweet grass or cedar is very pungent to those unaccustomed to it, but to the indigenous people it is a beautiful scent.

Native Nations have varied cleansing ceremonies, some involve washing in a river at dawn, dipping seven times, and others entail pain being inflicted upon the body. The cleansing ceremonies are as unique as the Nations who practice them.

What approach should be adopted by indigenous Christians in regard to these ceremonies? Like Paul they can continue practicing their traditional ceremonies, but they must honor them as one honors the sacrament of communion. Communion is not literally drinking the blood of Christ or eating his flesh, but rather, it is a symbolic act remembering the sacrificial death of Jesus on the cross. By drinking and eating, one symbolically partakes of His suffering and death.

With the smudge ceremony, one symbolically washes with the smoke, believing and thanking Creator Jesus for forgiveness and cleansing. 'But if we walk in the light, as he is in the light, we have fellowship with one another, and the blood of Jesus, his Son, purifies us from all sin' (1 Jn 1.7).

First Nations – Speak in their Heart Language
Many have felt they were on the outside of an inside joke? It is not a pleasant experience. Inside jokes are only fun for those on the inside who have the whole story and do not need background information.

Some of the greatest sermons one hears and remembers are those that include metaphoric language that relates to their culture. The opposite is also true; if one does not understand something, the message is a mystery. A pastor was giving an example of what Jesus can do in people's lives. He said, 'Jesus is like a snow plow'. The metaphor was lost on the Southern California congregation. One from northern Canada could immediately understand the comparison. During or after a snowstorm, the best place to be is behind a snowplow (a large truck that clears the highways of snow) because it is making the road safe.

There are many ways to get the attention of the indigenous people. Learn their stories and humor. If one can learn to speak in the heart language of any people, one will have their attention.

One of the author's fellow cohorts, Michael Palampo from Hope Chapel Mihilani, learned a greeting in the Carrier language the first time he met the author. He even continued to say, 'Hadih!' to the author, years later, and it was a great blessing and an honor to hear the Carrier language at The King's Seminary.

First Nations – let them know who they are

Every indigenous person knows how to introduce himself or herself to an audience. One begins by stating their tribal affiliation (Nation), where they are from (Reservation), and finally one's clan (if any) and a little about their family. At this point, the person describes the nature of their job. This sequence is very important for Native people. Where one is from defines one more than what one does. Once an Elder, who was a dear friend, needed a ride to the airport. Her brother was present. He never told the author his occupation but later the Elder said that he was a Chief. This is not false modesty but instead, reflects an unpretentious heart that does not need to be fulfilled by occupying a leadership position but can be at peace with who they are and their place in this world.

While many indigenous people acknowledge Jesus as God's Son because of early missionary efforts, many more teach their children to avoid Christians like the plague. They tell them that becoming a Christian means one will turn into a white person. They also teach how the church was responsible for attempting to eradicate their culture. In most cases, they are correct. So how can one bring Jesus to indigenous people in a manner that they will receive Him? One must be as thoughtful as the Apostle Paul was in his missionary dealings in the book of Acts.

The Apostle Paul's missionary efforts reveal a respect for other cultures. He explains that other cultures are worthy to receive the gospel but also indicates that no one culture is *the* holy culture. Paul does not feel it necessary to bring the gospel cloaked in Jewish culture. He continues to practice his cultural cleansing ceremonies even in the light of what the Cross accomplished for his salvation. Native people can therefore continue to practice their Native traditions, symbolizing the work of Jesus Christ on the cross, as much as they also dedicate babies to the Lord, are baptized, and take communion.

Anthropology

The anthropological point of view is 'Listen to the people'. Anthropology demands that people be described in their terms and not in terms of another. Columbus and every explorer, priest, and settler did the complete opposite. Native people deserve a right to convey whatever they believe and not be judged. The task of anthropologists, is to measure accurately what they hear and observe of any people group. Indigenous people deserve for their voices to be heard.

> The first step in ministry is to analyze different types of societies and cultures from a phenomenological or descriptive point of view. Our purpose is to understand them as those living in them do. We refer to this as an emic approach to the study of cultures. In an emic analysis, we must report accurately what people say. If people say that they speak with their ancestors, that women became pregnant by wading into a lagoon, and that shamans see spirits, we report these as facts that they believe to be true. This does not mean we agree with the ultimate truthfulness of what they say. Rather, it means this is what people believe and act on.

> It is important in this step to avoid passing judgment on people's beliefs until we understand them, at least in part. If we judge them, prematurely, we often jump to wrong conclusions. Moreover, if we pass critical judgments, people will not tell us their deeper beliefs for fear of ridicule.[89]

This Scripture shows that God can hear the prayer of nations who do not know about Jesus, '... In truth God shows no partiality. But in every nation whoever fears Him and works righteousness is accepted by Him' (Acts 10.34b-35, NKJV). This Biblical story is about Cornelius, and Peter speaks these words when he meets Cornelius, who was a God-fearing Gentile. The prayers of this God-fearing Greek lead to a mysterious man (Acts 10.30) dressed in shining clothes who instructs Cornelius to contact Peter. God was working on behalf of Cornelius, answering his prayers, even before Peter told him about Jesus. God then confirms His acceptance of this Gentile by baptizing him and all who hear the message (Acts 10.48).

Again, the message of this Scripture indicates that one can come alongside and walk with indigenous people toward Creator. Joining them on their path for a time does not disparage Christianity. It is

---

[89] Paul G. Hiebert and Eloise Hiebert Meneses, *Incarnational Ministry: Planting Churches in Band, Tribal, Peasant, and Urban Societies* (Grand Rapids: Baker Book House, 1995), pp. 14-15.

the way Jesus walked; eating and sitting with sinners, healing the sick and not bothering with the healthy.

High and low culture

There are several differences between Native people and non-Native people but the most fascinating is the distinction between high and low culture. Every culture has a method for processing information. How it is processed varies based upon the culture. American and Canadian cultures generally process information by explicit verbal instructions. This is Low-context Culture.[90] The term *low* is not derogatory but is used as quantitative (as in measurable). The cultural expectations are low and therefore the various aspects of every situation demand explanation.

Within High-context cultures, the cultural expectations are unspoken but individual responsibility is high. One does not need instruction in order to live within these High cultures, but does what is implicit. Indigenous societies are a High-context culture. The rules of engagement are completely unspoken but adhered to strictly.

> First, low-context cultures encourage communicators to separate the issue from the person, sometimes however, at the expense of personal relationships. Often, the rhetorical ideal of avoiding attacking the person is clearly the ideal: 'Just get the facts.' By contrast, high-context cultures tend not to separate the person from the issue. If you attack the issue, you are assumed to be attacking the person and would create embarrassment and ill will.[91]

Those from a Low-context culture are familiar with very direct communication, whereas those from a High-context culture are

---

[90] Carley H. Dodd, *Dynamics of Intercultural Communication* (Boston: McGraw-Hill, 5th edn, 1998), p. 90:

> American culture is considered to be on the low-context side ... For instance, some Americans use signs, instruction lists, and standard operating procedures ... Although there are numerous exceptions, in general, northern Europeans, western Europeans, and North Americans tend toward the low-context condition. Middle Easterners, Africans, and Latin Americans tend toward the high-context culture dimension, but somewhat less than Asian; Asians tend toward a high-context condition.

[91] Dodd, *Dynamics of Intercultural Communication*, p. 91.

122 Introduction to First Nations Ministry

more comfortable with indirect communication styles in order to promote group harmony.

Low-context cultured people do not like situations they do not understand. When they find themselves within a High-context culture, they can experience severe culture shock and become agitated or even angry. Low-context cultured people must ask many questions in order to feel secure in certain situations whereas people in High-context cultured people are very comfortable with silence and tend to know what is expected of them.

The next section is an indigenous reflection on the work of Paul Hiebert and Eloise Hiebert-Meneses.

Anthropology is a science. Christians throughout history have struggled with the intermingling of science and theology. Some have said that science has no place in theology largely because it throws shadows of doubt on their faith.[92] This approach leads to a dualism where people enjoy modern conveniences provided by science yet they do not allow science to inform their Christianity. Christians can also embrace this view when they affirm science over theology and thus undermine their faith in God.[93]

The second approach is compartmentalization. This stance asserts the belief that science is a matter of facts and truth and contrarily religion is a matter of feelings.[94] This dualism leaves healing to the medical doctors and views evangelism as a spiritual matter.

> A recent variation of this dualism is to use theology to define the gospel, but to use the methods of social and business sciences to grow churches. This approach fits that western worldview with its emphasis on human control, pragmatism, problem solving and doing something.[95]

Without science and theology in concert, one ends-up with a weak Christian faith and a trivial view of science.[96] The science of anthropology needs to inform missions. Of course, anthropologists are not perfect; they can disrupt life as badly as can conquistador

---

[92] Hiebert and Meneses, *Incarnational Ministry*, p. 10.

[93] Hiebert and Meneses, *Incarnational Ministry*, p. 10.

[94] Hiebert and Meneses, *Incarnational Ministry*, p. 11, this view of religion is Kantian philosophy.

[95] Hiebert and Meneses, *Incarnational Ministry*, p. 12.

[96] Hiebert and Meneses, *Incarnational Ministry*, p. 12.

missionaries. However, if they are faithful to their calling, they will tread carefully and do justly.

The final approach to science and theology is integration. "To describe human realities we need different maps, including theology, anthropology, sociology, psychology, biology, chemistry, and physics. Each contributes to our understanding of the whole.[97]

Hiebert suggests integration of science and theology as opposed to compartmentalization and reductionism. He states that it is ethnocentric and unacceptable for missionaries simply to apply their own worldview and judge all others based on their opinions. He suggests using comparisons to assess one's own ethnocentrism. Hiebert states that everyone's initial reaction is to assume the inherent rightness of his or her worldview, value, and judgment as *THE* correct one. Again, that is one's normal reaction, but it is very ethnocentric. Hiebert warns that, '... modern knowledge, too, is rooted in a worldview and that worldview, like all human worldviews, is flawed'.[98]

Hiebert also discerns that if one knows the gospel, but overlooks the fact that people live in contexts, they can misconstrue their culture for the gospel, thereby becoming a prejudiced judge of their culture. It has been proven that indigenous people will accept the gospel and non-indigenous culture, but it has also demonstrated to be ineffective among the majority of indigenous people who value their culture. The danger here is that the converts will become alienated[99] from their own people and the formation of a truly indigenous church is stunted. Rather Hiebert suggests, 'We need to understand the socio-cultural contexts of the people we serve'.[100] If this is done carefully, there should be no concern for the next paragraph.

The other danger is that one can lose sight of the gospel in an effort to understand and embrace human culture. Hiebert warns that if one makes the gospel into whatever one desires, then it loses

---

[97] Hiebert and Meneses, *Incarnational Ministry*, p. 13.

[98] Hiebert and Meneses, *Incarnational Ministry*, p. 16.

[99] Hiebert and Meneses, *Incarnational Ministry*, p. 18.

[100] Hiebert and Meneses, *Incarnational Ministry*, p. 18.

its transforming power, and one hears 'only the placating words of humans'.[101]

The root of the problem involving indigenous culture is that no Christian wants to err on the side of culture over the gospel. Therefore, 'when in doubt, throw it out', has been the motto of the missionary to Natives. However, this maxim should be thrown out. Of course, there are indigenous traditions that need the justice and mercy of God to change, but why are there *so many* elements in indigenous cultures that lend themselves to suspicion? The answer is simple: a person cannot accept what one does not understand. If there is no understanding and 'walking-alongside-of', then one will judge based on one's worldview criteria and this is unfair.

> We argue here for an incarnational approach to cross-cultural ministry. In this we make a distinction between human cultures and divine revelation given to us in Scripture. We realize, though that revelation must be expressed in specific cultural forms for us to understand it. This means that the Bible must be translated into different languages, and the Gospel expressed in thought forms and practices meaningful for people. It also means that the messenger must identify as closely as possible with the people she or he serves.[102]

God's Word casts a huge light onto one's life and culture and reveals areas where one is living right before God and areas where one has fallen short. Every culture includes sinful elements. This is as true of indigenous culture as it is of the Canadian and American. God's Word is a light that evidences that all sinners need salvation.

> It affirms that much in the culture we create is good, because it expresses God's image within us. It also declares much in our cultures and societies is evil, because we have made ourselves the gods of our own creations. There is both personal and corporate good and evil. Our response to human cultures must be an ongoing process of critical contextualization.[103]

---

[101] Hiebert and Meneses, *Incarnational Ministry*, p. 18.

[102] Hiebert and Meneses, *Incarnational Ministry*, p. 18.

[103] Hiebert and Meneses, *Incarnational Ministry*, p. 19.

It is only through critical contextualization that one determines what is good and of God, and what is not. This step should, however, never be taken without the consideration and assistance of the indigenous people themselves and also, perhaps a group who will work through the issues carefully and theologically. An undertaking of this magnitude would be a difficult task, however it is better than the alternative which has been accepting for too long – a group of white people instructing Native people as to what is good and what is not. That method is simply unacceptable.

> Transforming a society is a process. We must begin where the people are. We cannot expect new Christians to leave their old ways and adopt new ones instantaneously. Too often this is what we have tried to do in missions. But then we must lead people step by step in Christian faith and maturity in their own settings. We must help them also to study their own societies and cultures in the light of Scripture, and to charge their lives through the power of the Holy Spirit.[104]

In planting churches, ministering to indigenous people requires the utilization both of theological and scientific insights in order to determine how best to accomplish this work.[105] Hiebert tells readers to understand indigenous people from a 'phenomenological or descriptive point of view. One understands them as one living among them does.'[106]

Missionaries and believers in the Bible then utilize ontology to test these beliefs, otherwise everything is relative; 'every belief is treated as true and every cultural practice as good'.[107]

Anthropology accurately informs one's faith regarding contact with indigenous people. This project refers to this action as 'walking alongside indigenous people in their beliefs, on a journey towards Creator'. This is the simplest use of words to describe the tasks of anthropologists and missionaries if they want to be effective.

---

[104] Hiebert and Meneses, *Incarnational Ministry*, p. 19.

[105] Hiebert and Meneses, *Incarnational Ministry*, p. 14.

[106] Hiebert and Meneses, *Incarnational Ministry*, p. 14.

[107] Hiebert and Meneses, *Incarnational Ministry*, p. 15.

Conclusion

This review of relevant literature has evidenced through early church history, through modern anthropological methods, and through the words from the Bible referencing the missionary work of Paul to the Gentiles, that Native people deserve a second look. Native people have suffered long enough under erroneous stereotypes and the church is where healing must begin. The ancient wounds of the indigenous people of Canada and the United States run long and deep. The Church inflicted some of these wounds. Today the Church must begin the healing process by carefully listening to indigenous people and heaping honor to displace the layers of shame.

4

PROJECT METHODOLOGY

Rationale

This project is comprised of theological components and takes advantage of the writings of various indigenous and non-indigenous authors. These elements create the foundation for the project, which is to raise the awareness of indigenous ministry for non-Native pastors and leaders. The objective of this project is to further the work of the ministry among First Nations. The best way to further this ministry is for those involved to acquire a functional understanding of this unique ministry. Within indigenous ministry, many misunderstandings can impede outreach to First Nations and cause non-Native leaders to form unsuitable attitudes towards indigenous people and leaders. The effects of these mind sets may be completely oblivious to both the non-Native and the Native people, but if the hurtful attitudes exist, effective ministry will not occur. Often one does not recognize that they have made inaccurate assumptions about others because they do not take time to be conspicuous of their lack of knowledge. The crux of this project is to reveal the areas of misunderstanding so that a new relationship can be formed based on mutual trust and understanding.

Much of the misunderstanding with indigenous people has to do with different cultural value systems. Chapter 1 of this project illustrates how cultural values differ. The example given is of an overlooked Native leader. The Native leader does not step forward during a meeting to take charge but rather waits to be recognized. The unaware, non-Native pastor or leader could assume (and rightly so,

based upon their cultural underpinnings) that the Native leader is shy, not
a strong leader, non-assertive, not authoritative, maybe even afraid,
or they may not even notice the Native leader. Whereas the Native
community respects the Native leader's humility, which to them
displays honor.[1]

This scenario is continually played out (hundreds of times)
across the continent. Native leaders are overlooked for positions of
authority because those seeking to promote pastors and leaders select candidates through the lens of their own cultural criteria. They
tend to choose leaders who look and act the part, rather than an
indigenous leader who does not fit the mold.[2]

If it is to be effective and theologically valid, Native leadership
must be indigenous. Within Foursquare, there are great examples of
being attentive to indigenous leaders. Within the Canadian Foursquare Church[3] the National Board created the First Nations Affinity Unit. They created this Unit partially because of the events that
unfolded within Foursquare United States but mostly because of
their time spent with Native leaders. The author served on the National Board and was able to provide answers to many questions
regarding ministry to First Nations and related areas.

Native ministry in Foursquare USA was formerly under the Multicultural section and was not a separate District. At the time, Pastor
Ken Bringas was the leader of the Multicultural District of Foursquare Churches. One of the Native leaders in Foursquare, who
held an indigenous church meeting at The Church on the Way, disagreed with this decision. Bryan Brightcloud (Chiricahua Apache)
talked to the leadership within Foursquare and explained to them
that indigenous churches should not be under the Multicultural section because that area is involved with recent immigrant style

---

[1] Some non-Native leaders question the Native use of the word 'honor'. They
believe that only God deserves honor and one should not worry about honoring
people. This advice is often offered, but rarely followed. Most people frequently
display honor and offer respect. If a pastor is stopped for speeding on a freeway,
he or she does not believe they *need not* show respect and honor for the police
officer, but rather they will sometimes show an inordinate amount of respect in
order to beat the citation. Recognition and honor are a normal part of the Christian life, i.e. 'Honor your mother and father'.

[2] Of course, there are examples of Americans and Canadians who do not fit
the typical leadership mold and, unfortunately, they are overlooked as well.

[3] Formerly known as the Foursquare Gospel Church of Canada, renamed
when Pastor Barry Buzza became president in 2007.

churches. While Native Americans are cultural, they are not recent immigrants. Rather, those who are not indigenous are the immigrants. Instead of issuing demands to Foursquare leaders, Brightcloud asked Foursquare to bring together Native American leaders from across the nation to meet and discuss their future. After four such meetings, the Native leaders decided to create a new First Nations District in The Foursquare Church (USA). This action demonstrates that Foursquare does in fact listen and respond to indigenous leaders.

However, Chapter 3 of this project has shown that even the best of intentions can turn sour if one is not diligent with continued efforts to listen to the voice of the Native pastors and leaders. If the leadership of Foursquare does not tune a consistent ear toward indigenous ministry, they will miss many opportunities to bless and encourage Native ministry. Indigenous people never make decisions quickly but rather require time carefully to consider possible courses of action. There is also great value in bringing all the Native leaders together, not only for encouragement and for camaraderie, but also because decisions need to reflect a group consensus. This does not mean a gathering of a select group that will represent the larger body of pastors – it means everyone. Unfortunately, the total group appears more like a committee because there are so few indigenous churches in Foursquare Canada and United States. On the positive side, it will cost less for Foursquare to bring these Native leaders together. The comparatively few indigenous ministries and churches can be viewed in a positive light in that the ministry is in an embryonic stage and can therefore become something wonderful if non-Native leadership will listen to the voice of the indigenous pastors (*voice* is intentionally singular).

Chapter 3 also provided a strong argument against colonial type mission work among indigenous people. It argued that without using proper anthropological, missiological, and Biblical methods, the gospel will not take root and become the fundamental basis of the indigenous spiritual movement.

It has been argued in this project that if Canadians and Americans in Foursquare do not understand history from an indigenous perspective that they will not be able to understand today's indigenous people. Being honest about the past can bring justice to the future. First Nations people are weary of reconciliation services ending with an apology. Apologies are wonderful if both parties also work together toward restitution. Restitution precludes the reconciliation service from being a local public relations event. Thankfully, as far as the author knows, these types of events have not typically been a part of the Foursquare ethos.

Lastly, any missionary with a stereotypical view of indigenous people will have an impossible time relating and understanding the people and may wonder why years of work have resulted in such little fruit. The stereotype within the missionary may be unnoticeable to him or herself but will likely be recognized by the local Native people (who will never confront them because conflict is not part of the indigenous value system and is not a proper means of communication; although they may make jokes). The survey administered in this Seminar will greatly assist non-Native missionaries and pastors (working with Native people) in carefully examining their own heart. If they refuse to change their mind on any given issue it will signal a potential problem. In the historic past and unfortunately also the present, non-Native people have stereotyped Native people causing great anguish and anger. Therefore, it is inappropriate for those ministering to Native people to carry these stereotypes in their hearts into their ministry.

Procedures

The Introduction to First Nations Seminar consists of three parts. The first involves the initial survey, the second is a lecture based on the issues raised by the survey, and the third is a final survey (identical to the initial survey) revealing the growth, change, or lack thereof, in the perspective of the participants.

The First Survey involves ten statements requiring a *True, False, or Not-sure* answer. The goal is to eliminate any opportunity for neutral or ambivalent answers; however, an allowance is made for those who are 'not sure' of the answer. During the introduction to the seminar, participants are asked to avoid indecisive responses, if possible.

There is no preliminary coaching on the survey statements before the participants receive them. The only preparation they receive is the name of the Seminar itself: Introduction to First Nations Seminar, which is quite vague as to the content of the seminar and what would be expected of participants. The Seminars are conducted in classroom settings, and in every setting, the participants are made aware that the author is indigenous and there is also a brief time of worship. The author states that she would analyze the research data collected and publish the results, but that participants could enjoy confidentiality by remaining unnamed. The purpose of keeping the participants names confidential is to ensure that each person is comfortable in responding honestly to each statement, with no outside pressure.

There was some anxiety displayed on behalf of several of the participants, until they learned that their confidentiality was ensured, because as they apologetically admitted, they did not know much about indigenous peoples. However, after the author assured the attendees that this project would be of great value not only to the participants themselves, but also to the larger body of Christ, they were happy to take part. This process was interesting because not one person believed he or she was an expert on indigenous people. Some had experience with missionary work to indigenous people while others had no expertise whatsoever. There was also one separate test group comprised of twelve indigenous participants within one exclusive test group. All of the twelve indigenous leaders either attend Foursquare Churches or are involved in areas of leadership relating to the First Nations Unit in Canada. The Seminar was open to anyone regardless of nationality or ethnicity. The indigenous attendees may have influenced the results somewhat toward a deeper understanding of indigenous ministry; however, they account for only 11.8% of the participants. Most indigenous leaders, as well, said they had learned something.

The lecture format provides an overview of historical issues, theological questions, social classifications, and stereotypes that not only illuminates the wide-ranging assumptions made by non-Native leaders but also provides theological insight regarding their preconceptions. The presentation covers all ten statements on the Survey, individually addressing and, in turn, demystifying each presupposition. Two statements relate to historical integrity; two are theological in nature; four deal with social classifications and the final two consider stereotypes.

The methodology chapter addresses areas often misunderstood by non-Native people including stereotypes and assumptions; it also involves theological reflections.

The Introduction to First Nations Seminar transpired over the course of a year and involved 98 participants. The seminars varied in time depending upon the number of attendees. They lasted from one hour to three hours, with provision for breaks. The results of the Seminar are gleaned from a total of five Seminars, two were in Canada and three in the United States.

Mexico

The Introduction to First Nations Seminar was also conducted in Mexico. It will only be discussed in this section for purposes of conciseness and because this project was unfortunately limited to Canada and the United States. However, the Mexico Seminar results have a place in this project because they imply that the American church needs to look closely at the missions efforts within that country, not only to the indigenous peoples, but also to the Mexican people themselves. The Introduction to First Nations Seminar took place in 2007 at the Tijuana Foursquare headquarters with a gathering of thirty leaders during a District conference. Unfortunately, only 12 of the surveys were collected after the seminar but the comments from the seminar will be presented here. The plight of the indigenous people in Mexico, Central America, and South America deserves at least a cursory mention here as well as a brief summary of several Mexican pastors' perspectives of the Foursquare Church.

More indigenous people live in Mexico than in Canada and the United States combined. They deal with the same stereotypes, assumptions, social problems, and theological questions except on a larger scale. They are discriminated against not only by the government but also by the majority of Mexican people who believe the fairer one's skin the higher their class. They may not openly express this view, but it is an inherent part of the Mexican ethos. However, most of the celebrated Mexican culture is actually indigenous. Mexican food is actually indigenous food. Spanish people did not bring corn tortillas with chilies from Spain, this food came from the indigenous people. Indigenous people gave corn to the world. Every atrocity disclosed in this project and suffered by First Nations, can be magnified many times over when speaking of the indigenous people of Mexico. The experiences of the Native people in Canada and the United States have improved remarkably over the last century while not much has changed down South.

The Mexican pastors were more responsive than any other group to the Seminar. They were very grateful to have received this teaching and each one said it gave them a new perspective regarding indigenous people. Surprisingly, they related to the survey and lecture very personally. It reminded them of their difficulty as the Mexican Foursquare Church existing beside the United States. They felt that the Mexican Foursquare church is not always accepted as an equal ministry partner with the United States Foursquare Church. They perceive that ministry is often *done to them* rather than *with them* and they look forward to change.

Assessment Tools: The Surveys

Participants completed the initial survey prior to the seminar lecture and the final survey subsequent to the seminar lecture. The assessment tool itself is comprised of two surveys designed to address certain misunderstandings within Native ministry such as: Native worldview, values, spirituality; how Native people are perceived spiritually, ontologically, historically; and any stereotypical distortions.

The initial survey covers a plethora of issues surrounding misconceptions regarding indigenous peoples and the final survey measures any changes in one's comprehension of indigenous ministry. The goal of the two surveys is to analyze the participant's level of understanding of indigenous people before and after the lecture. The initial survey reveals the knowledge or the need for raised awareness while the final survey is a poll that measures the changes in perception of First Nations.

Figure 1. Survey – First Nations Issues

Read the following statements.
Please check whether you *agree*, *disagree*, or are *not sure*.

	Agree	Disagree	Not Sure
1. First Nations people arrived in the western hemisphere by a land bridge from Asia.	_____	_____	_____
2. First Nations are very similar to one another with some regional differences in dialect, culture, and customs.	_____	_____	_____
3. First Nations religions are animistic in nature	_____	_____	_____
4. First Nations societies were less developed than the nations of Europe.	_____	_____	_____
5. The First Nations were conquered by the superior warfare technology of the Europeans.	_____	_____	_____
6. In the late 1800's and early 1900's the First Nations population was double what it is today.	_____	_____	_____
7. Over the past 100 years the First Nations people have been slowly assimilating into the dominant culture.	_____	_____	_____
8. The 'Indian Reservation' system is basically a failure that has kept the First Nations people segregated and undeveloped.	_____	_____	_____
9. First Nations people have a genetic predisposition to alcoholism.	_____	_____	_____
10. The Federal Government provides many things free to First Nations	_____	_____	_____

The goal of the initial survey is to evaluate the extent of the knowledge the participants possess of indigenous people. Because the survey is to be used for ministry purposes, each statement is specifically designed to address certain misunderstandings within Native ministry such as: Native worldview, values, spirituality; how Native people are perceived spiritually, ontologically, historically; and any stereotypical distortions. The statements are similar to those in a book by Devon A. Mihesuah called, *American Indians: Stereotypes and Realities* (Atlanta: Clarity Press 1996). She wrote the definitive book on the stereotyping of Native peoples in the United States, gathering the stereotypes with which the Native people across the United States (and Canada) have for many years struggled, as evidenced even in Native ministry. Dr. Doug Pennoyer of Biola University, assigned this book to the author's husband in a class on Native American studies in 2007, just in time for it to be of assistance with this project. It succinctly defines many stereotypes and is a very relevant work. The author and her husband have also taught on these issues through First Nations Bible College since 1992.

Every indigenous person can compose a list of stereotypes because these issues are, unfortunately, a part of every day life for Native peoples. These stereotypes have been around for so long that sometimes indigenous people themselves believe in them. The reasoning behind the seminar is to shed light on these issues and to offer a convincing line of reasoning in opposition to each of them. There may be broad acceptance, or at least tolerance, of multiculturalism in larger cities but one-step outside the city is another world where misunderstanding (about indigenous issues) reigns.

The lecture discusses the initial survey statements and issues but exclusively *from an indigenous perspective.* This is a key point because most participants did not complete the survey with indigenous people in mind, they simply wrote what they knew or assumed about First Nations. The lecture reveals the indigenous perspective on all the survey statements and provides the accompanying rationale.

The three historical statements are numbers one, five, and six, with numbers five and six assessing whether participants believed that First Nations were a conquered people. Statement number one is a historical statement regarding the Bering Straight Theory and it also is a theological question. The Placement Theology section in Chapter 2 divulges the indigenous perspective on the Bering Straight theory while the stereotypes section in Chapter 3 addresses the 'conquered' statement.

The theological statements, numbers one and three, relate to the land bridge, which the Theology component (Chapter 2) of the project answers while the animistic statement is the most interesting of all as it is multi-layered and deserves a credible answer. The four statements relating to social classifications, numbers two, four, seven, and eight, address the following: 'Indian' implies one generic people; the nature of civilized indigenous culture; if assimilation strategies have worked; and if the reservation system was a bad idea? Finally, the last two statements, numbers nine and ten, deal with stereotypes. Statement number nine relates to indigenous predisposition to abuse alcohol while number ten assesses whether indigenous people get a free ride from the government. The statement regarding the propensity to abuse alcohol is refuted in the stereotypes section (Chapter 3) of this project.

After the lecture, the final survey was distributed. It consisted of a single-question asking if there was any change in the participant's perception of indigenous people. Participants were offered three choices, was their perception of First Nations greatly changed, changed, or not changed at all?

Summary

The Introduction to First Nations Seminar involved 98 participants from Canada (two seminars) and the United States (three seminars) over a period of two years (2006-2008). At the beginning of each three-part seminar, participants completed a specially designed initial survey. The initial survey tested the knowledge of non-Native participants regarding indigenous ministry (there were also 12 indigenous participants in one separate). Upon completion of the initial survey, the surveys were collected and placed in a manila folder for safekeeping.

The second segment of the seminar involved a lecture where the person conducting the seminar examined the validity of exact statement. From an indigenous perspective the answer to each question was 'Disagree'. The lecture included discussion of the statement in the survey, which was specifically designed to address certain misunderstandings within Native ministry such as Native worldview, values, spirituality; how Native people are perceived spiritually, ontologically, historically, and if there are any stereotypes.

The last part of the seminar was the final survey. This was a poll consisting of one question, the answers to which indicated whether participants had changed their perceptions of First Nations. Participants were asked the following question:

In your perception of First Nations at the Introduction to First Nations Seminar did you experience: (1) *A great change* in your perception of First Nations people, (2) *A change* in your perception of First Nations people, or (3) *No change* at all in your perception of First Nations people.

The results gathered from the initial and final surveys of the Introduction to First Nations Seminar are detailed in the subsequent chapter.

5

PROJECT RESULTS

Results of the Seminar Survey

This chapter records the results of the Introduction to First Nations Seminar. The goal of the Seminar and this project is to raise participants' awareness of their personal perceptions of First Nations worldview, ontology, values, spirituality, history, and stereotypes. The tools of measurement, which assessed any participants' awareness of First Nations Issues, included an initial survey, followed by a lecture and a final survey. The final survey polled the students to determine whether their perception of First Nations issues changed greatly, at all, or not at all.

The Initial Survey

This section of the project will detail the participants' answers to the initial survey administered in the Introduction to First Nations Seminar. The results garnered from the survey documents submitted by participants reveal a wide range of perceptions on First Nations issues.

There is no standard measuring device available to indicate the level of a person's knowledge about a particular people group. This measuring tool was developed[1] with specific questions in the areas of socio-economics, spirituality, history, stereotyping, ontology, and worldview. The initial survey is unique to the project, created specifically to interpret the extent of participants' understanding regarding First Nations issues.

---

[1] Initial Survey devised by Randy and Cheryl Bear-Barnetson, 2006.

The three historical survey statements are numbers one, five, and six, with statements five and six assessing whether participants believed that First Nations were a conquered people. Statement number one is a historical statement regarding the Bering Straight Theory. The Placement Theology section in Chapter 2 introduces the indigenous perspective on the Bering Straight theory while the stereotypes section in Chapter 3 addresses the 'conquered' statement.

The theological statements, numbers one and three, relate to the land bridge, which the Theology component (Chapter 2) of the project answers while the animistic statement is the most interesting of all as it is multi-layered and deserves a credible answer. The four statements relating to social classifications numbers two, four, seven, and eight, address the following: if 'Indian' implies one generic people; the nature of civilized indigenous culture; if assimilation strategies have worked; and if the reservation system was a bad idea? Finally, the last two statements, numbers nine and ten, deal with stereotypes. Statement number nine relates to indigenous predisposition to abuse alcohol while number ten addresses whether indigenous people get a free ride from the government. The statement regarding the propensity to abuse alcohol is refuted in the stereotypes section (Chapter 3) of this project.

Figure 2 establishes the initial survey responses of the ninety-eight participants.

Figure 2. Responses

1. History/Theology Statement – First Nations people arrived in the western hemisphere by a land bridge from Asia.

Agree: 44
Disagree: 22
Not sure: 32

2. Social Statement – First Nations are very similar to one another with some regional differences in dialect, culture, and customs.

Agree: 16
Disagree: 70
Not sure: 12

3. Theology Statement – First Nations religions are animistic in nature.

    Agree: 32
    Disagree: 34
    Not sure: 32

4. Social Statement – First Nations societies were less developed than the nations of Europe.

    Agree: 34
    Disagree: 54
    Not sure: 10

5. History Statement – First Nations were conquered by the superior warfare technology of the Europeans.

    Agree: 29
    Disagree: 53
    Not sure: 16

6. History Statement – In the late 1800's and early 1900's the First Nations population was double what it is today.

    Agree: 25
    Disagree: 24
    Not sure: 49

7. Social Statement – Over the past 100 years the First Nations people have been slowly assimilating into the dominant culture.

    Agree: 52
    Disagree: 25
    Not sure: 21

8. Social Statement – The 'Indian Reservation' system is basically a failure that has kept the First Nations people segregated and undeveloped.

    Agree: 39
    Disagree: 30
    Not sure: 29

9. Stereotype Statement – First Nations people have a genetic pre-disposition to alcoholism.

> Agree: 9
> Disagree: 58
> Not sure: 31

10. Stereotype Statement – The Federal Government provides many things free to First Nations.

> Agree: 21
> Disagree: 39
> Not sure: 38

Results from the Questions

The first statement on the Initial Survey relates to the history of First Nations people arriving in the western hemisphere by a land bridge from Asia. The survey asks if participants agreed, disagreed or were not sure. Of the 98 responses, 44 agreed with the statement, 22 disagreed and 32 were unsure. From an indigenous perspective, the correct answer is to **disagree**, because First Nations stories talk about Creator placing indigenous people on their land, giving it to them, not to own but to share and steward. The land bridge is a theory, which has caused nothing but grief to indigenous peoples. Native people consider it as an attack and even the term aboriginal denotes, 'you just arrived a bit before us'.

Statement two on the survey involves the social classification of generic indigenous identity. Statement two – First Nations are very similar to one another with some regional differences in dialects, culture, and customs. Some people believe that there is only one indigenous group. This statement received the highest percentage of correct responses with 70 participants in disagreement. Although one participant commented, *this is taught in public schools*, 16 participants agreed with the statement and 12 were not sure.

Statement three: 'First Nations religions are animistic[2] in nature'. The answers to this question were essentially split between those who agreed (32) and those who disagreed (34). This result reveals that most people do not understand indigenous spirituality.

Statement four addresses the social state of indigenous people before the Europeans arrived and whether the Native society was uncivilized (as compared to Europe). Only 34 participants agreed, while 54 disagreed, and only ten were not sure. This is an encouraging indication that some people understand certain elements of indigenous history and that there indeed was a civilized society here prior to contact with Europeans. The Potlatch people of the Northwest Coast had intricate societies as did many indigenous people. The problem with this question is the use of the term civilized because that is a relative term that can be used ethnocentrically. When traveling, most people tend to discredit the culture they visit because of their own ethnocentricity. From a missiological perspective, this attitude is very wrong.

Statement five relates to the First Nations being conquered by the superior warfare technology of the Europeans. The majority of participants answered this question correctly; only 29 agreed while 53 disagreed and 16 were unsure. The correct response to this statement is that First Nations were never conquered but rather their population was decimated by disease brought by the Europeans, and the skillful trickery that governments used to swindle Native land from First Nations. Most of the treaties have never been honored. Even today the indigenous people in Alberta, Saskatchewan, and Manitoba are fighting to keep their original agreements

---

[2] Winter and Hawthorne (eds.), *Perspectives on the World Christian Movement*, p. D-108. Regarding animism, Alan R. Tippett, *Introduction to Missiology* (Pasadena, CA: William Carey Library, 1987), p. 324, writes:

> The popular use of the term 'Animism' comes down to us from E.B. Tylor (1871). He did not give it the technical meaning it acquired from the comparative religionists, of 'a kind of religion,' but used it to signify 'the deep-lying doctrine of Spiritual Beings, which embodies the very essence of Spiritualistic as opposed to Materialistic philosophy.' It was, for him, 'a minimum definition of religion' which saw the animistic way of life as accepting the reality of spiritual force(s) and beings, over against the materialist outlook on life. 'In its full development,' Tylor agreed, it formulated concrete beliefs in such notions as the soul(s), the future state, controlling deities and subordinate spirits, especially when these beliefs result in 'some kind of active worship' (1871; I:425).

with the government. The government and large industries reinterpret agreements because of the huge oil resources on Native land.

Statement six is not a trick statement but one that tests what participants believe about the Native population today versus 100 years ago. Most participants did not realize that 100 years ago the Native people were almost wiped out. The population was nearly decimated; it was less than 50 percent of what it is today, but currently the population is rebounding.

Statement seven deals with assimilation. This socially related statement asserts that 'Over the past 100 years the First Nations people have been slowly assimilating into the dominant culture'. Unfortunately, 52 participants (53 percent) agreed with this statement, while only 25 disagreed and 20 were undecided.

The fact that the majority of participants agreed with the statement exemplifies the gap between what non-Native people and Native people believe. This response has implications for the church as well. If the majority of non-Native people believe that Native people are assimilating into the dominant culture, then they will not worry or even think about them missiologically. It will be normal simply to envelop the indigenous people into the larger church. However, the correct answer to this question is to disagree. There has been a revival of indigenous culture over approximately the last twenty years. Many Native people learned the stories of what transpired in the Residential Schools and they are aware of the assault that has taken place against the identity of Native people. More and more indigenous are returning to their traditional ways, learning their languages and being proud to be indigenous.

Some non-Native people mistakenly believe that indigenous people are similar to second and third generation immigrants who desire to become more American or Canadian, however, the opposite is true.

Statement eight is also social in nature and focuses on the reservation system. The statement holds that the system has been a failure by keeping Native people segregated and underdeveloped. Historically the reservations were a terrible idea and no Indian wanted any part of the arrangement because the army and governments were restricting Indian land more and more. Those acts worked terrible injustices on the Native people and today there are many unsettled land claims.

Project Results 145

Today Native people call the Reservation home. It is land and indigenous people are happy that they fought for their land and are now able to enjoy it When a Native person who lives in the city dies, they are taken home to their village to be buried.

Statement nine deals with stereotypes and speaks to the indigenous propensity to alcoholism. The stereotype section of Chapter 3 explains that Native people do not have a pre-disposition to alcoholism and the answers to the survey confirm that most people acknowledge this reality. The number of people who agree or are not sure is a little worrisome because it equates to 41 percent of the participants although 58 participants (59 percent) correctly disagreed.

The last statement, 'The Federal Government provides many things free to First Nations', addresses an additional stereotype. Twenty-one people (21 percent) agree with this statement. That is a significant percentage considering that 38 (39 percent) were unsure. Fortunately, 39 (40 percent) disagreed. The fact remains that most respondents are in the Agree or Not Sure categories, where they either believe this myth or are unsure. The truth is that Native people do not get 'many things' for free. What Native people receive is based on agreements made between nations, called treaties. If Native people get anything, it is more than likely that they got conned. Governments today have a number of successful strategies to employ against First Nations. One is that of delay, the other is the policy of moving ministers from one position to another. The government can delay answering people for years – even after the people involved are dead! Then they decide they do not have to answer.

Just when Native people get to know the new minister of the Indian Affairs department, they transfer him to another position, which results in the Native people being forced constantly to interface with the Institution as opposed to establishing a productive relationship with a person. As soon as a minister begins to understand and becomes sympathetic towards them, the official is relocated. The relationship with the government is strained at best. This, however, is part of the normal flow of life for most Canadians and American who can become very discontented with their government. The major difference in this instance is that the government has been taking undue advantage of Native people for many more years.

The Lecture

The second phase of the seminar involves a lecture, which addresses the issues discussed in the previous section. In addition to delineating the issues, the author presented the indigenous perspective and responded to each of the ten statements. From the First Nations perspective, the proper answer is to disagree with all of the statements. The lecture was approximately 45 minutes to 90 minutes in duration. The participants were able to understand clearly the thought processes of indigenous people regarding the statements and why they had differed in their responses.

The Final Survey

The final survey is a poll consisting of a single question. This is a poll of the participants to determine whether or not the Seminar changed their perception of First Nations. Participants were asked the following question:

> In your perception of First Nations at the Introduction to First Nations Seminar, subsequent to the initial survey and lecture, did you experience: (1) *A great change* in your perception of First Nations people, (2) *A change* in your perception of First Nations people, or (3) *No change* at all in your perception of First Nations people?

Here are the responses to the final survey question:

    Great Change 6
    Change   91
    No Change   1

The participant's answers to this question provided valuable insight as to whether the seminar was an impetus for change in the participant's perceptions of First Nations and to the degree of changed experienced. 99% percent of the participants experienced some degree of change in their perception of First Nations people. One person did not experience any change. This anomaly is not a negative since the individual is a non-Native leader who possesses a very strong grasp of First Nations perspectives. 'No change' in this instance simply means that the initial survey was correctly answered. The data compiled and presented in this chapter provides well-documented evidence that the First Nations Seminar was 100 percent effective in raising awareness of Native people. However, the overshadowing factor is that the evidence also demonstrates that there remains an on-going need to raise awareness in non-Native leaders.

Guidelines for the Assessment

The Introduction to First Nations Seminar has three integral parts. The first part of the Seminar is the most important because it documents the participants' views relating to various First Nations issues. After the administering of the initial survey, the lecture commenced. The lecture discussed the participants' responses to the ten statements and disclosed the indigenous perspective on all points. Upon completion of the lecture, the final survey question was presented to the participants. When the lecture was complete the participants were asked the final survey question. The results reveal that 99 percent of the participants experienced a change in their perception of First Nations.

The guidelines for the assessment of the seminar survey are based on first identifying points of disagreement. The initial survey contained statements reflecting conventional non-Native thought. The results clarify the gap that exists between the thought processes of non-Native people and Native people.

The results of the final survey were garnered by a single question poll, with a three-choice answer, at the conclusion of the Seminar. The goal of the project was to raise the general awareness of First Nations rather than to achieve an increase in perception on every single issue on the Initial Survey. This was convincingly accomplished.

Reflections from Participants

One participant's comment following the statement regarding First Nations coming over a land bridge reads, 'taught in public schools' under the checked 'agree' space while 'not sure' is checked with the note, '… as to truth'. This is a very poignant comment from a person who was obviously trying to think through this survey from an indigenous viewpoint.[3]

The majority of participants enthusiastically thanked the seminar lecturer/presenter regarding First Nations information and commented as to how much they had benefited.

Summary

The Introduction to First Nations Seminar was an overwhelming success. The initial survey revealed a degree of understanding among participants regarding several First Nations issues but more significantly exposed a serious lack of understanding on other very fundamental issues. The area of greatest concern involves assimilation. The majority of the participants wrongly assumed that First Nations are slowly being assimilated into American and Canadian culture. This response carries with it adverse implications for how non-Native leaders view Native people in their church.

---

[3] This quote is taken from a group where no indigenous people were involved.

6

REFLECTIONS

Response to Findings

The goal of this project is to raise awareness of First Nations issues. It is intended to measure the participants' increase in awareness of the issues addressed in each of the ten statements on the initial survey. The project accomplished the intended goal.

Did people advance in their understanding of a First Nation perspective? The statements are designed to confirm what non-Native people believe and think about First Nations and therefore to reveal the often-unknown misconceptions held by many non-Native leaders.

The initial survey solicited responses to ten statements pertaining to issues such as history, theology, social classification, and stereotypes which affect First Nations. It was not important whether a respondent believed the scientific theory of the Bering Straight; it was of consequence if they thought about the indigenous perspective of the Bering Straight. Only one person's comment, after checking the 'agree' response, suggested that he or she did not know the facts about the Bering Straight theory regarding indigenous migration.

Likely, the most relevant question to all people, regardless of nationality, is the question of spirituality. The survey worded this statement to echo what most non-Native people instinctively think about First Nations religion, that it is animistic and similar to Eastern religions.

This subject has been covered in the theology component of this project; however, it is appropriate to add several concluding remarks. Native people are not animists in the traditional definition of the word. While First Nations believe the earth is sacred, they do not worship nor they did they originally worship the Earth. First Nations have always believed in the Creator. The author has not yet discovered a First Nation that does not have a descriptive name for this Creator. There are many people who are skeptical about First Nations traditions and religion. Of course, there are aspects of every culture that are not acceptable, sanctified, or holy. Yet, for some reason, the indigenous ways are more suspect. People generally are more comfortable with sin when it arrives in their particular cultural package.

That First Nations and other Nations beliefs are not pure anymore is because of the darkening.[1] Of course, the darkening has impacted many other nations as well. One of the reasons there is so much pain between First Nations and non-Natives today is because non-Native Europeans believed that God had called them (the doctrine of Manifest Destiny), like Moses and Abraham out of persecution into the Promised Land. However, the analogy between the Canaanites and indigenous people is not helpful. Without question, the Canaanites allowed their hopes and dreams to guide their theology, which gave the Israelites the right to slaughter any in the way of their Promised Land and progress.

This project is very successful in raising awareness of the truth concerning indigenous beliefs. The church can embrace many Native traditions, especially the regalia, songs, and dances.

Interpretation of Results

The results of seminar show that there is a measure of comprehension on certain First Nations issues but there is still much room for improvement in understanding the indigenous side of the story. The results of the seminar demonstrate that it is quite common for participants to misunderstand indigenous culture, but also that there is remarkable understanding regarding some social and historical issues. The fact that misunderstanding remains is not attributa-

---

[1] The darkening is explained in the Placement Theology section in Chapter 2.

ble to the participants not caring about indigenous people, but rather is the fault of school history curriculum that focuses on the stereotypical aspects of history, the current use of Native mascots, and the fact that indigenous leaders are largely overlooked.

The seminar revealed non-Native people correctly understand that Native nations are different and that they consist of various groups. This realization is very encouraging.

Statement seven proved to be the most significant area of misconception. The majority of participants believe that First Nations are slowly being assimilated into the dominant culture. A majority of 52 participants agreed with this statement, while 25 disagreed and 21 were not sure. The *'not sure'* section is sizable and implies that there are more than 52 in agreement with this statement. These responses substantiate that there is a huge gap between what between what non-Native people and Native people believe. Most Native people are very proud of who they are, their people, where they come from, their unique language and history, and are able to glean what they need from the dominant culture without feeling any pressure or pressing need to assimilate.[2]

This unfounded belief regarding assimilation has daunting implications for the church. Why bother having indigenous churches if the Native people are assimilating? There is no need, right? Wrong, very wrong. There is a great need for indigenous churches led by indigenous leaders. There has been a revival of indigenous culture over approximately the last 20 years. Many Native people learned the stories of what occurred in the Residential Schools and they know the assault that has taken place against their identity. More and more indigenous people are returning to their traditional ways, learning their languages and being proud to be indigenous.

Some non-Native people mistakenly believe that indigenous people are like second and third generation immigrants who desire to become more American or Canadian, however, the opposite is true. The Native people need for their identity to be affirmed and strengthened. The revival of identity is a reality and Native people must also be affirmed as Native people in churches. They may not even recognize their need because it has been buried under shame

---

[2] Assimilate: (1) integrate: to integrate somebody into a larger group, so that differences are minimized or eliminated. (Microsoft: Encarta Dictionary, 2008).

and rejection for so many years. It is up to the church to bring heal-ing because the church was involved in the attempted assimilation and destruction of the indigenous identity.

The lack of understanding regarding assimilation means that non-Native people must learn proper missiological concepts and apply those to indigenous people here on American and Canadian soil. Unfortunately, they do not tend to think in these terms. Good missiology helps one to view the people in the mission field as equals, and not as requiring pity or in need of help. Good missiolo-gy demands that proper protocol is practiced when addressing dif-ferent people groups. Native people say we need to do this in a good way. The phrase 'in a good way' originated from the Native Elders who ask their people to walk with respect for all people, no matter their ethnicity or religion. Non-natives should speak to the chief before entering a village. If this practice is followed in the Amazon, then it should also be observed with the indigenous peo-ple in North America.

Summary of the Analyses

The answers to the final survey question revealed a need for non-Native people actively to attempt to understand the indigenous per-spective. The greatest need for education is in the area of the as-sumed assimilation of indigenous people.

Recommendations for Improving the Project

For future seminars, non-Native leaders will introduce and distrib-ute the initial survey. The survey results will be complied and the data available for the presenter at the outset of the lecture. When the presenter comes in to give the lecture, the answers on the initial survey will be accurate. When someone from a different culture in-terrupts a gathering of any people group, something changes in the atmosphere of the room.

Recommendations for Further Research

There are many aspects of this seminar that would benefit Four-square leaders. The seminar needs to be presented at Foursquare leadership gatherings. If the leaders do not understand the elementary details of indigenous ministry, how can one expect the church to be effective in First Nations ministry?

Some people might wonder why one would write such a seemingly biased project? Should an equivalent project be written to introduce Native people to the white culture?

Unfortunately, that experiment was already conducted through the Indian Boarding School/Residential School System and it failed miserably. Although students learned English and many other skills, the forced labor, the unfamiliar cultural expectations, the disapproval of their own traditional ways and language, the separation from the strong family circle, and the loneliness it caused provided irrefutable evidence that the Indian Boarding schools were a huge mistake.

Native people are cognizant of what knowledge is required to survive in the white world but they should not be required to change their inherent values and worldview in order to be accepted by the dominant society and institutions, especially the Church.

Another survey could be tailored to increase knowledge of indigenous people in Latin American leaders.

Recommendations for First Nations Ministry Application

Support for the Indigenous Leader

'There is no money in Native ministry.' This is a common slogan voiced by many pastors and leaders involved in Native ministry. Most pastors, missionaries, and leaders must find support from outside their own ministry because the church or mission does not bring in any tithes or local support. This seems to be true across the land.[3] Whether this is reasonable[4] or not will not be discussed here, it just happens to be the case.

---

[3] Meaning Canada and the USA.

[4] The goal of every ministry is supposedly to be 'self-sufficient' and yet there are mitigating factors that cause certain ministries in certain neighborhoods to be unable to support themselves. Just as there are members of families who are disabled and dependent on others for their well-being, there are churches in neighborhoods that are dysfunctional and cannot care for the church and pastor. Does that mean the church should move out of the area or that this neighborhood cannot benefit from a church and pastor? The reason God expects one to give to

The reality is that for indigenous ministry to be successful, it needs financial and spiritual support. Without assistance the indigenous ministry cannot stand. There need to be scholarships for First Nations at Pacific Life Bible College (Surrey, B.C., Canada) and Life Pacific Bible College (San Dimas, CA, United States). These scholarships can be distributed by the schools based on criteria provided by a group of indigenous Elders. These institutions also must recruit indigenous students. They must encourage the Native students in maintaining their identity and perhaps employ an indigenous counselor to mentor the students.

Indigenous ministry will not always require financial assistance. Native leaders are teaching their churches how to generate local support, but in the meantime, the churches will not be effective or even exist without outside aid.

The supervisor of the Unit/District must also receive financial support. This should include being compensated as a full time missionary because the work is in an embryonic state in the United States and Canada. The supervisor is forced to exist in two worlds, a challenging administrative role and as a pastor to pastors. The position deserves a full-time paid missionary's attention. This can be a bit confusing because the Supervisor appears to be more of a national leader. This is a great idea because indigenous people must be considered a mission field here in the United States and Canada. There are simply too many differences than cannot be mitigated. This concept has previously never been tested. Because all Native Nations are moving closer to autonomy and agree with the concept, it would be important for the church to release Native leaders. This paid position will not be overly financially advantageous to the missionary/national leader in any way because of the vastness of the country. This new structure must be considered if ministry to indigenous people is to be effective and lasting.

There is an unprecedented need among indigenous pastors to have a full-time supervisor who can travel to visit and encourage pastors. Who can understand the unique difficulties a Native pastor encounters on the Reservation or in an Urban center other than another indigenous pastor? The identity of indigenous people is very important and very different from Americans and Canadians.

---

the poor is because giving to the poor is the only time one gives and can expect nothing in return.

This cannot be overly stressed. Although most indigenous people speak English, the cultures, ways of being, and values are still very much indigenous and the people deserve to be treated as a foreign mission field.

There is a great need in our land for more indigenous ministry, especially from the Foursquare Church. Foursquare is a unique denomination that has many special attributes. These characteristics are significant in ministering to indigenous people, for example, the indigenous style church where people can actually look like who they are (e.g. Hawaiian shirts and the hula in a Hawaiian church), the embracing and encouraging of indigenous leadership, and especially their ability and desire to listen and learn about indigenous ministry from indigenous leaders. That is unique.

Trust

Earn Trust

In the past, missiological theory was used to justify a cultural genocide. In general, the early missionaries believed that everything in the indigenous culture was bad. However, Christ is transforming culture. In order to build-up the trust that has been lost because of the actions of non-Christian Native people, the church will need to do some hard work. Christ is above every culture not only the bad ones. Indigenous ministers who seek to contextualize the gospel for their people are often asked, 'What about syncretism?' This is a valid question, but it is not usually asked of churches in Canada and the United States. However, it is always asked of indigenous ministries. Every church has a culture and sometimes the culture of the church can become the focus of idolatry, especially when it takes precedence over relationship.

That huge barrier needs to be overcome if there is to be any development in the relationship between Natives and non-Natives. This is an issue when it comes to trusting indigenous leaders in positions of church governance and at the local church level when raising up and entrusting a Native leader in the church to become a minister. Some churches accomplish this very well and it seems that the Foursquare Church in the United States and Canada are on the right track, but further discussion is in order.

Recognize Differing Styles and Structure

Because indigenous people are different from the dominant cultures of Canada and the United States based on culture, traditions, religious beliefs, ontology, and political structure, it is very logical to allow indigenous leaders to develop and adopt indigenous ways of ministry. This includes the licensing of indigenous leaders, perhaps based more on a relationship model because giving Native leaders a number of papers to fill out is an insult. Because the quantity of papers is so overwhelming a barrier is erected between the supervisor and the leader.

Non-Native culture is very different from Native culture. Indigenous leaders can function in this foreign culture, but there are preferable ways to perform certain tasks that more appropriately fit their worldview and make better sense. These issues call for a gathering of indigenous leaders to create structures whereby indigenous people can enter the ministry in an indigenous way.

In addition, Native leaders are more evangelistic and are not always suited to remain in one specific location. These differing styles of leadership do not effectively mesh within the structure of the Foursquare church and therefore change is necessary. A few indigenous leaders have been lost because they did not fit the 'mold', meaning they were not comfortable remaining in one location. That is a great loss to Foursquare.

In addition, other structures, such as the Church Planning Institute, must be given a thorough overview to determine if they fit the indigenous people's way of being. Even Bible Colleges need to reserve space for indigenous students. There are many areas where Foursquare leadership would benefit from Native input in order to facilitate effective ministry to indigenous people.

The Call to Indigenous Ministry

Not everyone's worldview is made for missions, but that does not excuse the fact that we are called to 'Go into all the world and preach the gospel to all creation' (Mk 16.15, NKJV).

Questions to Answer if One is a Non-native Interested in Ministry to First Nations People:

  1. What is the indigenous nation nearest my city?

2. Are there any contextualized indigenous churches on the Reserve/Reservation? If so, then assist or join them. If not then proceed to step three. If they are not contextualized churches, find out why and walk alongside them to help them begin.

3. Meet the Chief. This is simply following protocol. Honor the Chief with a gift and ask if your Church can pray for them.

Summary

This chapter has addressed a number of very important and informative issues regarding ministry to indigenous people. For indigenous people, the most important issue is their identity. Where one is from (one's village, Reservation, Reserve) is of primary important and one's people group is a source of joy and pride. Indigenous people have many wonderful gifts to offer the body of Christ. Leaders such as Christina and Virgil Dawson who bring beauty, song, powerful words and rich stories, many tears, and much joy to any service, deserve to be recognized.

During a visit to Virginia, a Native leader related being the subject of an affront from a member of the dominant culture. A person said, 'You don't look like you are from around here. Where are you from?' The indigenous man said, 'I am Native American'. To which the questioner replied, 'I thought we killed you all off!' If the larger body of Christ can provide a setting where Native leadership can be observed and receive recognition, words like these will cease to sear the hearts of indigenous people.

Epilogue

The review of the Introduction to First Nations Ministry Seminar and the Literature Review revealed a deficiency of non-Native understanding of indigenous people. It is not.

Pastor Jack Hayford was sitting on an airplane beside a person and they struck a conversation. It turns out 'Bill' was a scientist of Kiowa ancestry.[5] After speaking with this man for a while, Pastor Jack felt God impress on him to speak in his spiritual language to

---

[5] Jack W. Hayford, *The Beauty of the Spiritual Language: My Journey Toward the Heart of God* (Dallas: Word Publishing, 1992), pp. 75-82.

Bill. Of course, Pastor Jack wanted to be sure of what God was asking him to do before he started. Again, he felt God impress, 'Speak to him in your spiritual language'. He began to speak in his spiritual language but the words that came out did not sound like the normal spiritual language with which Pastor Jack was familiar. The words were in a tongue that Bill immediately understood. He said they were old Kiowa words and they were very meaningful to him.

This story is meaningful to all because it illustrates that God is very interested in a personal relationship with each individual. God will speak in one's own language to each person. What is so significant to an indigenous person is that God spoke to Bill in his first language: the language of his heart. Historically one of the major identity attacks on the indigenous people of Canada and the United States was against indigenous language. God, speaking to this man in Kiowa reveals that God is not, and never was, interested in taking away one's language. On the contrary, God knew people's languages because He provided them.

Now God says to indigenous people through this story that although they were formerly rejected because of their ethnicity, God is showing His love to them through their own tongue. Just like the story from the Crow Elder, to speak in a Native tongue denotes authenticity. God spoke directly to this man's heart through his first language, the language of his heart.

Those who carry the gospel to indigenous people in Canada and the United States must be careful to be authentic in representing Christ (not just their cultural version), walking humbly before the Lord and before all people.

BIBLIOGRAPHY

Aland, Kurt, *Synopsis Quattuor Evangeliorum* (Stuttgart: Deutsche Bibelgesellschaft, 15th edn, 1996).

Alexander, Pat, *Eerdman's Handbook to the World's Religions: A Comprehensive Guide* (Grand Rapids: Eerdmans, 1994).

Anderson, Ray, *The Soul of Ministry: Forming Leaders for God's People* (Louisville, KY: Westminster John Knox Press, 1997).

—*The Shape of Practical Theology: Empowering Ministry with Theological Praxis* (Downers Grove, IL: InterVarsity Press, 1997).

Atwell, Robert (ed.), *Gregory of Nyssa: Spiritual Classics from the Early Church* (London: Church House, 1995).

Barram, Michael, *Mission and Moral Reflection in Paul* (New York: Peter Lang, 2006).

Berkhofer, Robert F. Jr., *The White Man's Indian: Images of the American Indian from Columbus to the Present* (New York: Vintage Books, 1979).

Bodley, John H., *Victims of Progress* (Mountain View, CA: Mayfield Publishing Company, 5th edn, 1999).

Bond, Laurel and Sandra Russell, *The Carrier of Long Ago* (Calgary, Alberta: Friesen and Sons, 1992).

Bothwell, Robert and J.L. Granatstein, *Our Century: The Canadian Journey* (Toronto: McArthur and Company, 2000).

Brash, Sara (ed.), *Defiant Chiefs* (Alexandria, VA: Time Life Books, 1997).

Brokensha, David, D.M. Warren, and Oswald Werner, *Indigenous Knowledge Systems and Development* (Washington DC: University Press of America, 1980).

Brown, Dee, *Bury My Heart At Wounded Knee: An Indian History of the American West* (New York: Henry Holt and Company, 1970).

Buller, Cornelius and Jonathan Dyck, 'Mapping The Land: Toward an Aboriginal Biblical Theology of Land', *Journal of North American Institute for Indigenous Theological Studies* 2.2 (2004), pp. 53-70.

Cassidy, James G. Jr., *Through Indian Eyes: The Untold Story of Native American Peoples* (Pleasantville, NY: Readers Digest Association, 1995).

Chalcraft, Edwin L., *Assimilation's Agent: My Life as a Superintendent in the Indian Boarding School System* (ed. Cary C. Collins; Lincoln, NE: University of Nebraska, 2004).

DeKorne, John C. (ed.), *Navaho and Zuni for Christ: Fifty Years of Indian Missions* (Grand Rapids, MI: Christian Reformed Board of Missions, 1947).

Deloria, Vine Jr., (Yankton Sioux), *Custer Died For Your Sins: An Indian Manifesto* (New York: The Macmillan Company, 1969).

—*God is Red* (New York: Dell Publishing Co., 1973).

DeYoung, Curtiss Paul *et al.*, *United by Faith: The Multiracial Congregation as an answer to the Problem of Race* (New York: Oxford University Press, 2003).

Dodd, Carley H., *Dynamics of Intercultural Communication* (Boston: McGraw Hill, 5th edn, 1998).

Duff, Wilson, *The Indian History of British Columbia: Volume 1, The Impact of the White Man* (Anthropology in British Columbia, Memoir. No. 5; Victoria, BC: Provincial Museum of British Columbia, 1964).

Duffield, Guy P. and N.M. Van Cleave, *Foundations of Pentecostal Theology* (Los Angeles: L.I.F.E. Bible College, 1987).

Elwell, Walter A., *Evangelical Dictionary of Theology* (Grand Rapids: Baker Books, 1984).

Fee, Gordon, *God's Empowering Presence* (Peabody, MA: Hendrickson, 2002).

—*Gospel and Spirit: Issues in New Testament Hermeneutics* (Peabody, MA: Hendrickson, 1991).

—*Listening to the Spirit in the Text* (Grand Rapids: Eerdmans, 2000).

—*Paul, the Spirit, and the People of God* (Peabody, MA: Hendrickson, 1996).

Fitzgerald, Michael Oren, *Indian Spirit* (Bloomington, IN: World Wisdom, 2003).

Fraser, Ian, *On The Rez* (New York: Picador USA, 2000).

Grentz, Stanley, *Theology for the Community of God* (Grand Rapids: Eerdmans, 1994).

Gross, Daniel R., *Peoples and Cultures of Native South America: An Anthropological Reader* (New York: Doubleday/The Natural History Press, 1973).

Guder, Darrell L. (ed.), *Missional Church: A Vision for the Sending of the Church in North America* (Grand Rapids: Eerdmans, 1998).

Hackel, Steven W., *Children of Coyote, Missionaries of Saint Francis: Indian-Spanish Relations in Colonial California, 1769-1850* (Othello, NC: University of North Carolina Press, 2005).

Harper, Walter (ed.), *Poems* (New York: W.W. Norton & Company, 1938).

Hausman, Gerald (ed.), *Prayer to the Great Mystery: The Uncollected Writings and Photography of Edward S. Curtis* (New York: St. Martin's Press, 1995).

Hayford, Jack W., *The Beauty of the Spiritual Language: My Journey Toward the Heart of God* (Dallas: Word Publishing, 1992).

—*Living the Spirit Formed Life* (Ventura, CA: Regal Books, 2001).

—*Pastors of Promise* (Ventura, CA: Regal Books, 2000).

Hazen-Hammond, Susan, *Through the Centuries with Mother Earth and Father Sky: Timelines of Native American History* (New York: The Berkley Publishing Group, 1997).

Hiebert, Paul G., *Anthropological Insights for Missionaries* (Grand Rapids: Baker Book House, 1985).

—*Anthropological Reflections on Missiological Issues* (Grand Rapids: Baker Book House, 1994).

—*Christian Missions and Modern Culture: Missiological Implications of Epistemological Shifts: Affirming Truth in a Modern/Postmodern World* (Harrisburg, PA: Trinity Press International, 1999).

—*Cultural Anthropology* (Grand Rapids: Baker Book House, 1983).

Hiebert, Paul G. and Eloise Hiebert Meneses, *Incarnational Ministry: Planting Churches in Band, Tribal, Peasant, and Urban Societies* (Grand Rapids: Baker Book House, 1995).

Hoeft, Karen, 'Community Capacity Development in an Aboriginal/Inuit Context', *Journal of North American Institute for Indigenous Theological Studies* 2.2 (2004), pp. 71-88.

Holt, Bradley P., *Thirsty for God: A Brief History of Christian Spirituality* (Minneapolis, MN: Fortress Press, 2005)

Hughes, Lotte, *The No-Nonsense Guide to Indigenous Peoples* (Toronto, ON: New Internationalist Publications, 2003).

Hultkrantz, Ake, *The Religions of the American Indians* (Berkeley, CA: University of California Press, 1979).

Hunhndorf, Shari M., *Going Native: Indians in the American Cultural Imagination* (New York: Cornell University Press, 2001).

Hultkrantz, Ake, *The Religions of the American Indians* (Berkeley, CA: University of California Press, 1979).

Jenkins, Philip, *The Next Christendom: The Coming of Global Christianity* (New York: Oxford University Press, 2002).

Josephy, Alvin M. Jr., *The American Heritage Book of Indians* (New York: The American Heritage Publishing Co., 1961).

Kidd, D.A., *Collins Latin Gem Dictionary* (London: Collins, 1966).

Klug, Lyn, *Soul Weavings: A Gathering of Women's Prayers* (Minneapolis: Augsburg, 1996).

Kraft, Charles H., *Anthropology for Christian Witness* (Maryknoll, NY: Orbis Books, 1996).

—*Communication Theory for Christian Witness* (Maryknoll, NY: Orbis Books, 2005).

—*Culture, Communication and Christianity: A Selection of Writings by Charles H. Kraft* (Pasadena: William Cary Library Books, 2001).

Kraft, Marguerite G., *Understanding Spiritual Power: A Forgotten Dimension of Cross-Cultural Mission and Ministry* (Maryknoll, NY: Orbis Books, 1995).

Kroeber, A.L., *Handbook of the Indians of California* (New York: Dover Publications, 1976).

Lachs, Samuel Tobias, *A Rabbinic Commentary on the New Testament: The Gospels of Matthew, Mark and Luke* (Hoboken, NJ: Ktav Publishing House, 1987).

Ladd, George Eldon, *A Theology of the New Testament* (Grand Rapids: Eerdmans, 1993).

—*The Gospel of the Kingdom* (Grand Rapids: Eerdmans, 1959).

Landes, Ruth, *The Ojibwa Woman: Male and Female life cycles among the Ojibwa Indians of Western Ontario* (New York: W.W. Norton & Company, 1938).

Lingenfelter, Sherwood G. and Marivin K. Mayers, *Ministering Cross-Culturally: An Incarnational Model for Personal Relationships* (Grand Rapids: Baker Book House, 2nd edn, 2003).

Loewen, Jacob A., *Culture and Human Values: Christian Intervention in Anthropological Perspective* (Pasadena, CA: William Carey Library, 1975).

Maclean, John, *Native tribes of Canada* (Toronto: William Briggs, 1896).

Matthiessen, Peter, *In The Spirit Of Crazy Horse* (New York: Viking Penguin, 1991).

Maxwell, John, *Developing the Leaders around You* (Nashville: Thomas Nelson, 1995).

McFadyen, Alistair, *The Call to Personhood* (Cambridge: Cambridge University Press, 1990).

Muller, Hugo, *Why Don't You? A Look at Attitudes towards Indians* (Toronto: Anglican Publications, 1972).

Murphy, Terence and Roberto Perin, *A Concise History of Christianity in Canada* (Don Mills: Oxford University Press, 1996).

Nerburn, Kent, *The Wisdom of the Native Americans* (Novato, CA: New World Library, 1999).

Newbigin, Lesslie, *Missionary Theologian: A Reader* (compiled by Paul Weston; Grand Rapids: Eerdmans, 2006).

Noll, Mark A., *A History of Christianity in the United States and Canada* (Grand Rapids: Eerdmans, 1992).

Oden, Thomas, *Pastoral Theology: Essentials of Ministry* (San Francisco: Harper Collins, 1983).

Oswalt, Wendell H., *This Land Was Theirs: A Study of Native North Americans* (New York: Oxford University Press, 8th edn, 2006).

Pearce, Roy Harvey, *Savagism and Civilization: A Study of the Indian and the American Mind* (Berkeley: University of California Press, 1988).

Pearlman, Myer, *Knowing the Doctrines of the Bible* (Springfield: Gospel Publishing House, 1937).

Peterson, Eugene, *The Message: The Bible in Contemporary Language* (Colorado Springs, MO: NavPress, 2002).

Piper, John, *Let the Nations Be Glad: The Supremacy of God in Missions* (Grand Rapids: Baker Academic, 2nd edn, 2003).

Pritzker, Barry M., *A Native American Encyclopedica: History, Culture, and Peoples* (New York: Oxford University Press, 2000).

Progoff, Ira, *The Cloud of Unknowing* (New York: Dell Publishing Co., 1983).

Ritchie, Mark Andrew, *Spirit of the Rainforest: A Yanomamo Shaman's Story* (Chicago: Island Lake Press, 2nd edn, 2000).

Schaff, Anne Wilson, *Native Wisdom for White Minds: Daily Reflections Inspired by the Native Peoples of the World* (New York: Ballantine Books, 1995).

Schobinger, Juan, *The First Americans* (Grand Rapids: Eerdmans, 1994).

Shelley, Bruce L., *Church History In Plain Language* (Dallas: Word Publishing, updated 2nd edn, 1995).

Shubin, Russell G., 'That the Natives Might Lift Jesus Up: A Conversation with Richard Twiss', *Mission Frontiers* 22.4 (September 2000), pp. 8-11.

Spence, Lewi, *Mythe of the North American Indians* (New York: Gramercy Books, 1994).

Stott, John (ed.), *Making Christ Known: Historic Mission Documents from the Lausanne Movement, 1974-1989* (Grand Rapids: Eerdmans, 1996).

Tedlock, Barbara and Dennis Tedlock, *Teaching from the American Earth: Indian Religion and Philosophy (Reissued)* (New York: Liveright Publishing Corporation, 1992).

Thompson, Laura, *The Secret of Culture: Nine Community Studies* (New York: Random House, 1969).

Unni, Mohanan, 'Marketplace Ministry: Context for the Praxis of Spiritual Growth and Affirmation for the Laos of God' (DMin project, The King's Seminary, 2006).

Utter, Jack, *American Indians: Answers to Today's Questions* (Norman: University of Oklahoma, 2nd edn, 2001).

Winter, Ralph D. and Steven C. Hawthorne (eds.), *Perspectives on the World Christian Movement: A Reader* (Pasadena: William Carey Library, 1992).

Wright, N.T., *What Saint Paul Really Said* (Grand Rapids: Eerdmans, 1997).

Zimmerman, Larry J., *Native North America: Belief and Ritual, Visionaries, Holy People, and Tricksters, Spirits of the Earth and Sky* (London: Duncan Baird Publishers, 1996).

Journals

Furniss, Elizabeth, 'Pioneers, Progress, and the Myth of the Frontier: The Landscape of Public History in Rural British Columbia', *BC Studies* 115/116 (Autumn/Winter 1997/98), pp. 7-44. *BC Studies* is a quarterly journal published under the auspices of the University of British Columbia, Vancouver, BC, Canada.

Provan, Iain, 'The Land is Mine and You Are Only Tenants (Leviticus 25:23): Earth-keeping and People-keeping in the Old Testament' *CRUX* 42.2 (Summer 2006), pp. 3-16.

White, Lynn Townsend Jr., 'The Historical Roots of Our Ecologic Crisis', *Science* 155.3767 (March 10, 1967), pp. 1203-207.

Indigenous Authors (includes Journals and Books)

Aldred, Ray (Cree), 'Us Talking To Us', *Journal of North American Institute for Indigenous Theological Studies* 1.1 (2003), pp. 79-93.

—'The Resurrection Story', *Journal of North American Institute for Indigenous Theological Studies* 2.2 (2004), pp. 5-14.

Alexie, Sherman (Spokane), *Indian Killer* (New York: Warner Books, 1996).

Fee, Anders C., *Chief Joseph: The Biography of a Great Indian* (New York: Wilson-Erickson, 1936).

Bear Heart (Muskogee Creek), *The Wind is my Mother: The Life and Teachings of a Native American Shaman* (New York: Berkley Books, 1999).

Blaisdell, Bob (ed.), *Great Speeches by Native Americans* (New York: Dover Publications, 2000).

Bruchac, Joseph (Abenaki), *Eagle Song* (New York: Puffin Books, 1997).

Champagne, Duane (Turtly Mountain Chippewa) (ed.), *Contemporary Native American Cultural Issues* (Walnut Creek, CA: AltaMira Press, 1999).

Church, Casey (Potawatomi), 'Authentic Christian Education from a Native American Point of View', *Journal of North American Institute for Indigenous Theological Studies* 3 (2004), pp. 81-94.

Crow Dog, Mary (Lakota Sioux), *Lakota Woman* (New York: Harper/Perennial, 1990).

Deloria, Phillip J. (Yankton Sioux), *Playing Indian* (Newhaven, CT: Yale University Press, 1998).

Deloria, Vine Jr. (Yankton Sioux), *Custer Died For Your Sins: An Indian Manifesto* (New York: The Macmillan Company, 1969).

—*For This Land: Writings on Religion in America* (New York: Routledge, 1999).

—*God is Red* (New York: Dell Publishing, 1973).

Dyck, Jonathan and Cornelius Buller, 'Mapping the Land: Toward an Aboriginal Biblical Theology of Land', *Journal of North American Institute for Indigenous Theological Studies* 2.2 (2004), p. 68.

Eastman, Charles A. (Lakota Sioux), *The Soul of the Indian: An Interpretation* (Lincoln, NE: University of Nebraska Press, 1911).

Erasmus, Peter (Cree), *Buffalo Days and Nights* (As told to Henry Thompson) (Calgary, Alberta: Fifth House, 1999).

Fixico, Donal L. (Seminole/Muscogee Creek), *The American Indian Mind In A Linear World: American Indian Studies and Traditional Knowledge* (New York: Routledge, 2003).

Hall, Lizzette (Carrier), *The Carrier, My People* (Cloverdale, BC: Friesen Printers, 1992).

Jacobs, Adrian (Cayuga: Six Nations), *Aboriginal Christianity: The Way It Was Meant to Be* (Rapid City, SD: Adrian Jacobs, 1988).

—'Drumming, Dancing, Chanting, and Other Christian Things: Getting Beyond the Fear of Syncretism and Facing the Challenge of the Sanctification of Native American Culture', *Mission Frontiers* 22.4 (September 2000), pp. 16-18.

—'Vulnerability and Mentoring', *Journal of North American Institute for Indigenous Theological Studies* 1.1 (2003), pp. 167-71.

—*Pagan Prophets and Heathen Believers: Native American Believers in the God of the Bible* (Rapid City, SD: Adrian Jacobs, c 1999).

—'Toward Indigenous Education Evaluative Standards', *Journal of North American Institute for Indigenous Theological Studies* 3 (2005), pp. 71-80.

Jaimes, M. Annette (ed.), *The State of Native America: Genocide, Colonization, and Resistance* (A Race and Resistance Series; Boston: South End Press, 1992).

Jean, Terri (un-enrolled Powhatan), *365 Days of Walking the Red Road: The Native American Path to Leading a Spiritual Life Every Day* (Avon, MA: Adams Media Corporation, 2003).

Jolly, Joseph (Cree), *Going and Growing Through Grief: Understanding the Grieving Process* (Moose Factory, Ontario: Mocreebec Council of the Cree Nation Health Program, 2000).

Kidwell, Clara Sue, Homer Noley, and George E. Tinker. (Osage/Cherokee), *A Native American Theology* (Maryknoll, NY: Orbis Books, 2005).

LaRose, Ed (Pomo), *Our Trail of Tears: A Journey of Reconciliation* (Scotland, PA: Healing The Land Publishing, 2006).

LeBlanc, Terry (Micmaq), 'Compassionate Community ... or Unchecked Greed? Two Views on Economic Development', *Mission Frontiers* 22.4 (September 2000), p. 21.

Margolin, Malcolm (ed.), *The Way We Lived: California Indian Stories, Songs, and Reminiscences* (Berkeley, CA: Heyday Books & California Historical Society, 1981).

McLuhan, T.C. (ed.), *Touch the Earth: A Self-Portrait of Indian Existence* (New York: Promontory Press, 1971).

Mihesuah, Devon A. (Choctaw), *American Indians: Stereotypes and Realities* (Atlanta: Clarity Press, 1996).

—*Natives and Academics: Researching and Writing about American Indians* (Lincoln, NE: University of Nebraska Press, 1998).

Momaday, N. Scott (Kiowa), *House Made of Dawn* (New York: Harper/Perennial, 1999).

Moore, MariJo (Cherokee) (ed.), *Genocide of the Mind: New Native American Writing* (New York: Thunder's Mouth Press/Nation Books, 2003).

Moran, Bridget (as told to her by Mary John, Carrier), *Stoney Creek Woman: Sai'k'uz Ts'eke: The Story of Mary John* (Vancouver, BC: Tillacum Library, 1988).

Olson, Sylvia (with Rita Morris and Ann Sam. Both Coast Salish), *No Time to Say Goodbye: Children's Stories of Kuper Island Residential School* (Victoria, BC: Sono Nis Press, 2001).

Peters, Spence (By various children of British Columbia), *The Legend of the Flood: Tales from the Longhouse* (Sidney, BC: BC Indian Arts Society, Gray's Publishing, 1973).

Qaumaniq (Cherokee/Inuit) and Suuqiina (Inuit), *Warfare by Honor: The Restoration of Honor: A Protocol Handbook* (Chambersburg, PA: Healing the Land Publishing, 2005).

Russell, George (Saginaw Chippewa), *American Indian Facts of Life: A Profile of Today's Population, Tribes and Reservations* (Phoenix: Native Data Network, 2004).

Smith, Craig Stephen (Chippewa), *White Man's Gospel* (Winnipeg, Manitoba: Indian Life Books, 1997).

—*Writing the Cross Culture: Native Fiction on the White Man's Religion* (Golden, CO: Fulcrum Publishing, 2006).

Tinker, George E., *Missionary Conquest: The Gospel and Native American Cultural Genocide* (Minneapolis: Fortress Press, 1993).

—*Spirit and Resistance: Political Theology and American Indian Liberation* (Minneapolis: Augsburg Fortress, 2004).

Treat, James (ed.), *Native and Christian: Indigenous Voices on Religious Identity in the United States and Canada* (New York: Routledge, 1996).

Twiss, Richard (Rosebud Sioux), *One Church Many Tribes: Following the Way God Made You* (Ventura, CA: Regal Books, 2000).

—*Syncretism: Some Biblical and Missiological Definitions: A Redemptive Approach to the Issue of First Nations Cultural Expressions of Worship and Christian Faith* (Vancouver, WA: Richard Twiss, 1998).

—'Out of Sight, Out of Mind', *Mission Frontiers* 22.4 (September 2000), pp. 12-13.

Waters, Anne (ed.), *American Indian Thought: Philosophical Essays* (Oxford, UK: Blackwell Publishing, 2004).

Woodley, Edith (Shosone) and Randy Woodley (Keetoowah Cherokee), 'Ministry in a good way: A new model for Native American Ministry',

Journal of North American Institute for Indigenous Theological Studies 2.2 (2004), pp. 15-28.

Woodley, Randy (Keetoowah Cherokee), *Living In Color* (Grand Rapids: Baker Book House, 2001).

—*Mixed Blood Not Mixed Up: Finding God-given Identity In A Multi-Cultural World* (Randy Woodley, 2000).

—'Putting It to the Test: A Look At Congregations That Are Aiming To Worship With Native Forms', *Mission Frontiers* 22 (September 2000), pp. 18-19.

—*When Going to Church is Sin: And Other Essays on Native American Christian Missions* (Scotland, PA: Healing the Land Publishers, 2007).

Bibles

The New International Compact Reference Bible (Grand Rapids: Zondervan Publishing House, 1998).

E-Form

From Indian and Northern Affairs Canada website:
http://www.ainc-inac.gc.ca/ch/rcap/sg/sg23_e.html
http://www.cstc.bc.ca/cstc/82/residential+schools
http://www.afn.ca/article.asp?id=57

INDEX OF BIBLICAL REFERENCES

INDEX OF AUTHORS

Made in the USA
Las Vegas, NV
24 February 2023